STEPHEN
HAWKING

Physicist and Educator

Bernard Ryan, Jr.

Ferguson
An imprint of ☑®Facts On File

Stephen Hawking: Physicist and Educator

Ferguson
An imprint of Facts On File, Inc.
132 West 31st Street
New York NY 10001

Library of Congress Cataloging-in-Publication Data
Ryan, Bernard, 1923–
    Stephen Hawking: physicist and educator / Bernard Ryan, Jr.
        p. cm
    Includes index.
    ISBN 0-8160-5546-7 (hc: acid-free paper)
    1. Hawking, S. W. (Stephen W.)   2. Physicists—Great Britain—Biography.   I. Title.
    QC16.H33R93 2004
    530′.092—dc22   2004001748

Ferguson books are available at special discounts when purchased in bulk quantities for businesses, associations, institutions, or sales promotions. Please call our Special Sales Department in New York at (212) 967-8800 or (800) 322-8755.

You can find Ferguson on the World Wide Web at http://www.fergpubco.com

Text design by David Strelecky

Pages 107–137 adapted from *Ferguson's Encyclopedia of Careers and Vocational Guidance, Twelfth Edition*

Printed in the United States of America

MP Hermitage 10 9 8 7 6 5 4 3 2 1

This book is printed on acid-free paper.

CONTENTS

1

"IN SOME WAY DIFFERENT"

In Aspen, Colorado, in August 1995, some 1,500 music lovers were thrilled to greet an unusual master of ceremonies at a major outdoor concert. Most of the crowd considered Aspen a favorite place not only for music festivals but for meetings of leading physicists. Now they were enthusiastically applauding a master of ceremonies (MC) who could not walk onto the stage. He rolled into view in a motorized wheelchair in which he slumped rather than sat. As their applause quieted, they knew the frail, motionless man in the wheelchair could not speak, yet he was being honored with the opportunity to introduce the musical numbers on the program.

The voice they heard was synthetic: sounds created by a computer attached to the arm of the MC's wheelchair.

Stephen Hawking is the most famous scientist alive today.
(Campix)

"This is the *Siefried Idyll*," said the steady monotone, "which Wagner wrote in 1870 to be performed on Christmas morning outside the bedroom of his new wife. I am here with my fiancée, Elaine, and we will be married in September, so I think this piece is rather appropriate."

The MC was Stephen Hawking, the most famous scientist of his time. He was a man whose body had suffered for 53 years with ALS (amyotrophic lateral sclerosis), known as Lou Gehrig's disease, but whose mind had provided answers to many of the questions about how our universe works. He was a leading physicist and the world's foremost expert in cosmology—the study of the origin, structure, and relationships to space and time of the Earth and everything beyond it.

Son of a Doctor

Stephen William Hawking was born in Oxford, England, on January 8, 1942, the 300th anniversary of the death of Italian astronomer and physicist Galileo Galilei. Stephen's father, Frank Hawking, was a doctor who had specialized in tropical diseases in East Africa. The outbreak of World War II in 1939 had drawn Frank Hawking home expecting military service, but authorities valued him more as a medical researcher. In that job, he met and married a medical secretary who became Isobel Hawking. Stephen was the first of their four children.

Following the war, Frank Hawking became head of the division of parasitology at England's National Institute of Medical Research. When Stephen was eight, his family moved to St. Albans, a prosperous middle-class town. There in 1952 Stephen passed entrance exams for the local private school, St. Albans School. Like other students, he wore a school uniform and cap. He appeared to be the kind of skinny little kid who was often teased and sometimes bullied. He had an awkward, unclear manner of speaking that his few friends dubbed Hawkingese.

Dr. Frank Hawking and his son, Stephen, in 1942 (Campix)

Within three years, teachers at St. Albans knew that Stephen was bright, but his marks stayed only just above average. With friends who were also known as smart kids, Stephen listened to classical music programs on BBC radio and attended concerts at the Royal Albert Hall. They rode their bicycles far into the countryside, and they spent long hours playing complex board games for which Stephen invented the rules.

"Awkward questions I can't answer"

By the time Stephen was 12, one of his friends later recalled, "I realized for the first time that he was in some way different and not just bright, not just clever, not just original, but exceptional." Another friend remembered that Stephen was always taking things apart—clocks, radios, anything mechanical or electronic—to see how they worked. This friend recalled that 14-year-old Stephen seldom spent much time on homework, yet "while I would be worrying away at a complicated mathematical solution to a problem, he just knew the answer—he didn't have to think about it."

Stephen and his classmates were taken on field trips to museums and factories. At one chemical plant, a scientist who had been conducting their tour took the teacher aside after Stephen had asked some questions. "Who . . . have you got here?" asked the scientist. "They're asking me all sorts of bloody awkward questions I can't answer!"

As a boy, Stephen lived and attended school in St. Albans.
(Campix)

Planning His Future

Looking ahead toward college, Stephen decided to concentrate on mathematics and physics during his last two years in St. Albans School. (Unlike American high school students, many British students decide on a college major while in the 11th grade.) His father assured him the only future in math was in teaching. He thought his son should plan a career in medicine, which would require more chemistry courses than Stephen wanted to take. After many arguments, Stephen agreed to study some chemistry as well as math and physics in St. Albans, but not to make any commitment to medicine.

By the time he was 16, Stephen and his friends were rounding up parts from clocks and a telephone switchboard to build their own computer. Stephen's mind worked out the design, while his pals, whose hands were better coordinated than his, took care of assembling the machine. They named it the Logical Uniselector Computing Engine (LUCE) and proved—as a local newspaper, the *Herts Advertiser*, reported—that it could answer certain mathematical questions. (The LUCE would be a valuable museum item today if only a computer teacher at St. Albans School had not tossed into the trash a box marked *LUCE*. It contained what he thought was just a mess of old wires and transistors.)

Stephen wanted to follow in his father's college footsteps by going to University College, one of 35 colleges within Oxford University. To get in, he had to pass two days of entrance tests: two exams in physics, two in math, and one in world issues and current affairs. Each exam lasted two and a half hours. Then came two sets of interviews. The first was with four deans and tutors who mainly wanted to find out what kind of person the applicant was. The second was with a specialist who wanted to find out how much he knew about physics.

Before the onset of his illness, Stephen was as physically active as any other boy. (Campix)

Within two weeks, Stephen was accepted for entrance at Oxford in October 1959. He did not know that he had received a 95 percent grade on both physics tests and only slightly lower marks on the other three exams. He did know, however, he was offered a scholarship.

2

LIFE AT OXFORD

At 17, Stephen Hawking was one of the youngest students at University College, Oxford University's oldest college, which dates from 1249. No friends from St. Albans went with him. Many other students at Oxford had performed military service before college and were several years older than he was, so Stephen's college social life was lonely; college work, as far as he was concerned, was a bore.

Each week in the Oxford curriculum, students were expected to attend several lectures as well as one tutorial—a small group of students led by a young professor or graduate student in a discussion of problems assigned the week before. One week, Dr. Robert Berman, who was Stephen's adviser, assigned 13 problems to his four physics students. On the morning of the tutorial a week later, the other three students told Stephen that two of them had managed to do one and a half problems, while the third student had completed just one. Hawking said he had not yet looked at the problems. The others went off to lectures while Stephen, skipping the morning's lectures, went to his room to tackle the physics problems. At lunchtime, just before the tutorial, one of the friends asked Stephen how many he had done. "I've only had time," he replied, "to do the first nine."

"I think at that point," said one of the other students a few years later, "we realized that it was not just that we weren't in the same street [as Stephen], we weren't on the same planet."

Another tutor, Patrick Sanders, assigned some problems from a textbook. Stephen returned the next week to say that he had done none of the problems but had marked all the errors in the textbook. He then spent 20 minutes of the tutorial explaining the errors, convincing the awestruck Sanders that the student knew far more about the subject than the teacher knew.

Hawking's mentor and adviser, Dr. Berman, summed up his analysis of Stephen's aptitude: "Undergraduate physics was simply not a challenge for him. He did very little work, really, because anything that was do-able he could do. It was only necessary for him to know something could be done, and he could do it without looking to see how other people did it."

Physics: The Big and the Little

When Stephen Hawking entered college, he knew that the field of physics consisted of two distinct areas of study: general relativity and quantum physics.

General relativity explained what went on in the vast cosmos beyond our sky. Basically, it was Albert Einstein's brainchild. Einstein had started in 1905 by declaring that physicists should think of space and time not as two separate things but as two parts of a whole, which he called spacetime.

After more than 10 years' work, Einstein published his general theory in 1916. It said that as beams of light move through spacetime and pass close to the sun, they are bent because the presence of any object in space distorts the spacetime around it. Thus, the pull of the sun's gravity bends the light coming to us from a star and changes the way we see the position of the star. Einstein was proved right three years later, in 1919, when photographs taken during a total eclipse—with the sun's brilliant light hidden—revealed just what he had described. In a word, Einstein was saying that what we see in space is relative to certain facts about space and time.

At about the same time as Einstein was expressing his theory of relativity, astronomer Edwin Hubble used an extremely powerful new telescope to make a surprising discovery: The countless galaxies beyond our own Milky

Way Galaxy are all moving away from one another. Within our Milky Way or any other single galaxy, however, the stars are not moving farther apart, but entire galaxies are.

Reviewing Hubble's findings, some physicists who specialized in the cosmos agreed that if the galaxies were moving apart, at some time eons ago they must have been close together, perhaps so close they touched or were a single something in space. To explain what started everything moving apart, physicists came up with the idea that there must have been a super-explosion of that original something. Not all physicists agreed, however. One such physicist, named Fred Hoyle, thought he was poking fun as he called that explosion a *Big Bang*. The name stuck.

While some physicists were all wrapped up in questions of general relativity, others were looking into the tiniest of the tiny particles that make up all matter. Their thinking involved what they called the *quantum theory*, and their discoveries became known as the *quantum revolution*. They found, for example, that although light seems to flow in a steady stream of energy, it is actually a series of extremely small particles, which they labeled *photons*. Photons are carried in waves.

Stephen knew that heat, ultraviolet rays, infrared rays, X rays, radio waves, and cosmic rays are other types of energy transmitted in waves described as radiant energy. He also knew that all matter is made of tiny units called

Stephen at his graduation from Oxford University (Campix)

atoms. Inside any atom is a nucleus made of protons and neutrons, with electrons moving in orbits around the nucleus. Any atom is capable of absorbing energy or giving off energy (absorption or radiation, respectively). The quantum theory, also called quantum mechanics, is the study of how this happens.

Because any tiny particle in the quantum world consists of waves of energy, Stephen knew that nobody could say exactly where such a particle was at any given moment. This fact had led a German physicist named Werner Heisenberg to his *uncertainty principle*. Stated back in the 1920s, it said that nobody could figure out all the characteristics of a quantum particle such as an electron. Rather, a physicist can only determine the particle's most likely *probabilities*.

A River Changes Stephen's Personality

Stephen's undergraduate days at Oxford were taking him deep into the study of both general relativity and quantum physics, but he found himself bored and unchallenged. At the same time, after a year or so of little social activity, he discovered a centuries-old Oxford tradition: the sport of rowing (also called crew).

Stephen was not built with the powerful physique of the oarsmen who pulled oars in unison to propel sleek, narrow shells (a type of boat) along the water. But his strong voice and light weight made him an ideal coxswain—the member of the crew who sits at the stern of the shell and controls its rudder while shouting orders and encouragement to the eight oarsmen. Stephen could be counted on to show up in good weather or bad, hot or cold, at dawn or dusk, for practice rowing.

University College's coach of crew, Norman Dix, thought Hawking was a skilled coxswain but noticed that he showed no interest in trying to become coxswain of the first boat, the varsity crew. Stephen also had a daredevil way of sometimes steering his boat through gaps so narrow the shell returned to the boathouse with its oar blades damaged. "Half the time I got the distinct impression," Dix later recalled, "that he was sitting in the stern of the boat with his head in the stars, working out his mathematical formulae."

Being a crew coxswain changed both Stephen's personality and his social life. He became a popular member of the in crowd, enjoying parties and participating in boisterous practical jokes after strenuous rowing practices. When he went home to St. Albans during holidays, old friends welcomed not the awkward schoolboy they remembered but a confident 19-year-old college man who knew how to have fun.

Unlike American undergraduates, who attend four-year colleges, British students go to university for three years. In the spring of 1962, Stephen was getting ready for final exams. He knew he could expect tough questions. And he figured out that in his three years at University College, Oxford, he had studied or worked about one hour per day, which was nowhere near the time his classmates had spent. He also knew that the exam papers would give him a wide choice of questions. He could select only those that posed problems in the theories of physics, ignoring questions about facts that he had not studied or memorized. He went into the finals ready to let his natural understanding of physics guide him through.

Stephen also wanted to earn top marks because he was applying to Cambridge University to study for a Ph.D., and he couldn't get into Cambridge without a first-class honors degree from Oxford. The marks he earned, however, put him just below a first-class degree but above a second-class. That meant he had to face a personal interview with university examiners.

The Oxford board of examiners knew Stephen Hawking as a brilliant but difficult student. They knew of his devotion to rowing, and they knew he had managed to skip one undergraduate lecture after another. They recognized his sometimes shabby appearance, his often-apparent laziness, and his preference for beer and fun rather than reading and writing assignments. After a number of questions, the chief examiner asked Stephen to explain his plans to the examining board.

"If you award me a first [honors degree]," said Stephen, "I will go to Cambridge. If I receive a second, I shall stay in Oxford, so I expect you will give me a first." And that is what they did.

3

CANES AND QUASARS

During his final months at Oxford, Stephen noticed that he often bumped into things while walking. Tying his shoelaces seemed to be more and more difficult. Sometimes his legs suddenly collapsed under him, and his speech would slur for no apparent reason. He took his concern about these minor difficulties with him to Cambridge in the fall of 1962 without telling anyone about them.

Studying at Cambridge

Stephen's main interest on arriving at Cambridge University was cosmological research, for he had decided he would rather study the vast universe than concentrate on the smallest of the small. "I thought that elementary particles were less attractive," he later wrote, "because, although they were finding lots of new particles, there was no proper theory of elementary particles. All they could do was arrange the particles in families, like in botany. In cosmology, on the other hand, there was a well-defined theory—Einstein's general theory of relativity."

Stephen hoped to study under the noted astronomer Fred Hoyle, whose worldwide reputation made him Cambridge's leading cosmologist. Instead, his mentor became Dennis Sciama, a professor who, unlike Hoyle (who was always traveling to meetings and speaking engagements), was close to his students. Stephen soon made a lifelong friend of Dr. Sciama, who was not only an inspiring adviser but an outstanding scientist. Only the year before, Sciama had become the only professor in England to teach relativity.

Stephen soon became one of Sciama's Cambridge graduate students who were thinking hard about cosmology. They knew that, while the Big Bang theory had been around for some 40 years, most physicists just did not believe in it. Rather, they believed in the *steady-state theory*. It assumed that, while the universe expanded and galaxies moved apart, matter developed from nothing and created new galaxies to replace those that died off, so the universe was always more or less the same, or steady.

Dr. Sciama believed in the steady-state theory. So did Fred Hoyle, who had jokingly invented the term *Big Bang*.

Parents See Something Wrong

Stephen went home to St. Albans for Christmas vacation. His parents, who had not seen him for months, noticed immediately that something was wrong. His speech was slurred, his motions awkward. Ice-skating with his mother, he fell down and couldn't get up by himself. At a family New Year's Eve party, guests saw him pouring wine but mostly missing the glass and splashing the tablecloth. At the same party, Stephen met a St. Albans high school senior named Jane Wilde. Together, they chatted the old year into the new.

Fearing that his son had multiple sclerosis, a disease that affects the central nervous system, Dr. Hawking put Stephen into the hospital for two weeks of tests. Stephen was soon diagnosed with amyotrophic lateral sclerosis (ALS), known in the United States as Lou Gehrig's disease and in England as motor neuron disease.

There is no cure for ALS. In its course, the muscles atrophy, or wither, so the victim loses mobility and becomes paralyzed. In most cases, death comes, usually within two years, from pneumonia or suffocation on the loss of respiratory muscle function. Meantime, the disease is painless and the mind remains clear and unaffected. At 21, Stephen was much younger than most people who are diagnosed with ALS.

Back in Cambridge and following doctors' advice to continue his studies, Hawking went through a period of deep depression. But he thought about a boy who had died of leukemia in the bed opposite him in the hospital. "Clearly there were people who were worse off than me," he later said. "At least my condition didn't make me feel sick. Whenever I feel inclined to be sorry for myself, I remember that boy."

He also thought about how he had chosen a field of study in which all his work would be done in his brain, which could not be affected by ALS. And his new friend from New Year's Eve, Jane Wilde, was becoming a close and dear companion who already accepted the dreadful fact of his ALS. Thinking about his life to come, he decided that "if I were going to die anyway, it might as well do some good." More seriously than ever before, Stephen decided to concentrate on his work.

"I worked it out."

By the spring of 1963, Stephen was using a cane and having more and more difficulty getting around. He often arrived at classes with his head bandaged as the result of a fall. Yet he insisted on going wherever and doing whatever he pleased. One evening he made his way to a meeting of the Royal Society in London. There, in a speech to about 100 leading scientists, Fred Hoyle announced his latest mathematical findings on the origin of the universe. He ended by asking if anyone had questions.

Hawking struggled to his feet. "The quantity you're talking about," he said, "diverges."

Murmurs rippled through the crowd of distinguished scientists. If this young man was right, they knew, Fred Hoyle's latest findings had to be wrong.

"Of course it doesn't diverge," replied Hoyle.

The murmuring stopped. "It does," said Stephen.

Everyone could see Hoyle's exasperation. "How do you know?" he responded.

"Because," said Stephen in his slow, slurring way, "I worked it out."

The upshot was that Hoyle accused Hawking of unethical and unprofessional conduct in making such a charge in a public meeting. In turn, Hawking accused Hoyle of unethical conduct in announcing theories that had not been verified by others. Stephen then wrote a paper that proved that he was correct and that Hoyle had been in too big a hurry to make his findings public. The event made graduate student Stephen Hawking a notable name in cosmology.

New Discoveries

In 1963, Stephen and many other graduate students heard exciting news about the work of astronomer Maarten

Schmidt at the Mount Palomar Observatory in California. For several years, Schmidt and others had observed light waves and radio waves coming from some things, most of which were more distant than any known galaxies. Schmidt and his associates felt that these sources could not be considered stars but might be called quasi-stellar objects, or *quasars,* as they were later known.

Quasars, Stephen learned as he studied Schmidt's work, have vast powers of energy. Condensed into a space about the size of our solar system, any quasar contains at least 100 million times the mass of our sun. It is busily sucking vast amounts of matter into a huge and hot whirling confusion, a process that physicists find impossible to describe. In effect, the process swallows stars, and many physicists then called the effect "collapsing stars." (Several years later, quasars were to be named "black holes.") This activity produces such enormous amounts of energy that a quasar's light waves can be as strong as those from 300 billion suns—bright enough for astronomers to see them across billions of light years of space. And its radio waves, too, can be picked up by powerful radio telescopes.

Dr. Hawking

Over the next year or so, Stephen and Jane saw more and more of each other, knew they were in love, and became engaged to be married. Writing later about Stephen, Jane said, "He was very, very determined, very ambitious. He already had the beginnings of the condition when I first knew him, so I've never known a fit, able-bodied Stephen."

Jane Hawking (Campix)

Stephen's determination included refusing help. His fellow graduate students remember, for example, a trip to London for a meeting when they all dashed late to board a train and saw Stephen struggling along the platform with his two canes. With the train about to depart, they hesitated to go out and help him aboard, for they knew how much he disliked being treated as disabled. But they did go out and help him.

On one such trip to London, Stephen met Roger Penrose, an outstanding mathematician who had been a student of Dr. Sciama's. In talks at King's College in London, Stephen heard Penrose discuss his theory on points in spacetime that were presumed to be infinitely dense. Penrose called such points *singularities.* Penrose used complex mathematical equations to prove that when a star collapsed, it became a singularity. At the center of any of those vast, whirling, confusing quasars, he said, a space-time singularity would be found.

During the train ride home from one of Penrose's meetings, Stephen turned to his mentor, Dr. Sciama. "I wonder what would happen," he said, "if you applied Roger's singularity theory to the entire universe." Dr. Sciama advised Stephen to make that question the basis of his Ph.D. thesis.

Stephen went to work. He thought, What if the universe as it expands is doing just the opposite of what a star does as it collapses? If a star can become a single point of infinite density in a quasar, why can't the whole universe have begun as a single point of infinite density—a singularity?

The last chapter of Stephen's dissertation astounded the Cambridge examiners who reviewed it. "There is a singularity in our past," he wrote simply. Then he proceeded with a brilliant theory, backed up with mathematical equations that the examiners found remarkable. After reading that chapter, they awarded the 23-year-old cosmologist his Ph.D. He became Dr. Stephen Hawking.

4

MARRIED LIFE AND PULSARS

Stephen and Jane wanted to get married soon after he received his Ph.D. But first Stephen needed a job. He applied for and won a fellowship at one of Cambridge's colleges, Caius (pronounced *keys*). There he would continue his research in theoretical physics.

Honeymoon and a New Home

Stephen and Jane were married on July 15, 1965, and went to Suffolk for a week's honeymoon. Then they were off to the United States for a summer program in general relativity at Cornell University in Ithaca, New York. The honeymoon ended abruptly when the newlyweds found themselves living in a dormitory reserved for young families. The shared kitchen offered no pots or pans, and the hallways vibrated with the babble and screams of toddlers. A new acquaintance drove Jane to downtown Ithaca to buy a few basic kitchen utensils, since the Hawkings, like most other students, could not afford to dine out.

Stephen had now lived longer than the two-year expectancy for most people who have ALS, but his condition continued to worsen. Walking with two canes was more and more of a struggle. Fortunately, back again in Cambridge, he and Jane managed to find a house for rent that was very close to Stephen's office in the department of applied mathematics and theoretical physics (DAMTP). The house was a tiny, cozy old building with ceilings so low that tall visitors had to duck through the doorways. This was to be their home for many years, and the enthusiastic Hawkings welcomed guests at any time. Jane herself was still a student, majoring in modern languages at Westfield College.

Revisiting the Big Bang

For cosmologists, these were busy, challenging days. Some of them were beginning to realize that the entire universe—not just our Milky Way Galaxy, which includes 100 billion stars, but everything in space—might be a singular vast quasar. Einstein had figured out that extremely long rays of light could be bent by gravity. Perhaps the universe itself held light rays that orbited from the edge, or horizon, of this quasar and went round and round, bent by spacetime so they returned again and again. In effect, spacetime might very well be bent around itself.

Thinking further, Stephen and his associates wondered whether this enormous example of spacetime we call the universe might be a quasar in reverse, expanding matter outward rather than sucking matter into its vortex. They discussed the Big Bang theory and the questions of people who, scoffing, asked what existed before the Big Bang. They knew that equations worked out by Einstein proved Hubble's observations that space was expanding and carrying the galaxies along with it. So it made sense that about 15 billion years ago there must have been a singularity that included all matter as well as time, energy, and space.

When that singularity exploded, the physicists figured, its temperature for one-tenth of a second was 30 billion degrees Celsius. The explosion mixed material particles (such as electrons, protons, and neutrons) and high-energy radiation. Three minutes later, the whole universe was 70 times hotter than the sun's center is today. The universe then cooled for 700,000 years until it reached the temperature of the sun's surface today and stable atoms could be formed by nuclei and electrons.

For nearly 15 billion years since then, the small group of cosmologists agreed, gravity has been at work gathering clouds of gas in space while electrons, protons, and neutrons have held together to form stars and galaxies.

Just as Stephen, Roger Penrose, and a few others were puzzling this out, they learned in 1965 that radio telescopes at Bell Laboratories in New Jersey had picked up microwave radiation. The waves' temperature proved that the radiation had to be left over from the Big Bang. The discovery turned the scoffers and doubters into serious students of the Big Bang theory.

A Full Life and an International Audience

Two things were now happening. Stephen was living a full and loving married life with Jane, refusing to give in to the difficulties of ALS. And he was concentrating, with Roger Penrose, on working out a new mathematical procedure that could prove the existence of a singularity at the beginning of time. They were confident that, if the general theory of relativity correctly describes the universe, their theory about the singularity had to be right.

In December 1965 Stephen was invited to speak at a week-long meeting on relativity in Miami, Florida. Jane went with him, and at the conference they caught up with an old friend, George Ellis, and his wife, Sue. The Ellises were spending a year at the University of Texas in Austin, where George worked with America's leading cosmologists. Because Stephen's severely slurred speech was now hard for most people to understand, Ellis agreed to deliver Stephen's talk on singularity theory for him. The audience of leading scientists from around the world listened eagerly and warmly accepted Stephen's theories.

During a free afternoon at the conference, the two couples enjoyed basking in the sunshine on the hotel's private beach. But at dinnertime they discovered locked beach gates kept them from returning to the hotel. The Ellises found a kitchen window open in the hotel's side wall, climbed in, and went to work helping Jane to lift in Stephen's awkward body. As they struggled, some Spanish-speaking employees of the hotel gawked at the weird effort. Jane, a modern-languages major, used her fluent Spanish to explain what was going on. The workers joined in, got Stephen through the window, and led the couples back to their rooms.

By the summer of 1966, Stephen could no longer manage to walk with two canes. Now he used crutches. His father had been studying ALS and developed a progression of vitamins and steroids that was to help his son during the next 20 years. Meantime, Jane finished her college work, typed Stephen's Ph.D. thesis, and managed their tiny household, which was still a busy center of social activity.

The Hawkings' dinner parties saw loud and lively discussions not only of theoretical physics but of current events and gossip while equally loud classical music blared from the record player. Often, the evening ended with lingering guests holding their urge to help as the determined Stephen, heading upstairs to bed, took 15 minutes or more to struggle all by himself up the winding stairway.

All the Hawkings' friends admired Stephen's confident attitude and cheery disposition in the face of a physical condition that would discourage anyone else. His DAMTP and Cambridge associates, at the same time, were sometimes astonished at his challenging and outspoken attitude at work. He was one of those people whose minds quickly and relentlessly dig into the assertions of even the most prominent authorities. He was never hesitant about asking embarrassing questions.

Stephen's hard work brought him a prominent award in 1966, when he won the well-respected Adams Prize for his essay "Singularities and the Geometry of Spacetime." It added to his growing worldwide reputation as a cosmologist.

Fatherhood and New Discoveries

Stephen and Jane became parents on May 28, 1967, when Robert George Hawking was born. Apparently inheriting his father's determination, Robert arrived two weeks ahead of schedule. The new life in the household seemed to add to the ALS patient's stamina. "It obviously gave

Stephen a great new impetus," said Jane, "being responsible for this tiny creature."

With the arrival of the baby, Stephen and Jane had to consider whether they should continue renting their tiny home or look for one to purchase. They had been happy in their house, however, and it was ideally located near Stephen's workplace. They happily discovered that the owner was willing to sell the house and a building society was willing to grant them a mortgage. Stephen's father helped with money for improvements, and friends arrived to apply paint and fresh wallpaper to the Hawking family's own cozy home.

Around this time, Stephen became aware of a huge development in his field. While astronomers at Cambridge were testing a new radio telescope, they discovered radio waves that flashed on and off with striking precision several times per second. Some, in fact, flashed several hundred times a second. Someone called the phenomenon a pulsating radio source, and the phrase was shortly reduced to the word *pulsar*.

Twenty-five-year-old Stephen Hawking and his Cambridge colleagues spent several months analyzing the discovery. They knew the pulses had to come from a very compact star that was either vibrating or rotating. They finally figured out that the cause was something that had been predicted in theory for 30 years but that no one had paid much attention to: The pulses were neutron stars within our galaxy and rotating. These stars came from the explosions of giant stars called supernovas. In effect, a pulsar was a collapsed star whose spacetime was so entirely wrapped around itself that its light waves, or photons, could not escape into the outside universe. Because no light could get out, the American cosmologist John Wheeler called such a collapsed star a *black hole*.

5

FAMILY LIFE AND BLACK HOLES

By 1970, Stephen's family and friends were able to convince him that he could get around better in a wheelchair than on crutches. He accepted the chair but never the idea that he was, to use a word he strongly disliked, handicapped. He still insisted on going where he wanted to go and doing what he wanted to do. And he wanted his family and friends to act accordingly. Jane put it this way: "Stephen doesn't make any concessions to his illness, and I don't make any concessions to him."

A New Addition and a New Position

On November 2, 1970, Jane gave birth to a baby girl, whom Jane and Stephen named Lucy. Her father had now been invited to join the staff of the Institute of

Jane and Stephen Hawking on the campus of Cambridge University (Campix)

Astronomy, which was too long a wheelchair ride from the Hawking home. To get to work three mornings a week, Stephen got a permanent loan of a little blue three-wheeled vehicle called an "invalid car" from the National Health Service. He drove it himself. On the other two days a week, he continued to work in his office near home at the DAMTP. He soon became established in his own office at the institute, attracting prominent theoretical physicists and astronomers from around the world to his conferences and readings of papers.

One night soon after Lucy was born, Stephen was thinking about black holes as he was getting ready for bed. "My disability makes this rather a slow process," he later said, "so I had plenty of time. Suddenly, I realised that many of the techniques that Penrose and I had developed to prove singularities could be applied to black holes." He was so excited he could hardly sleep.

Early next morning, he phoned Penrose. If nothing can escape from a black hole, he said, that means its mass can never get any smaller. But if radiation or matter of some kind fell into the hole, its surface area would always increase. Even if two black holes collided, the new black hole would have an area greater, or maybe the same as, the sum of the areas of the original two.

Thinking about Heat and Cold

Over many months, Hawking and Penrose thought about thermodynamics (the study of how heat moves) and entropy (a physics word for the way all matter and energy in the universe, even solid rocks, eventually decay and become inert). Thinking deeply in quantum physics, they worked at developing complex mathematical formulas and writing papers for such publications as *Communications in Mathematical Physics.* They debated whether the temperature of a black hole is absolute zero and whether radiation could escape from the hole. Throughout 1973, they thought it could not.

Early in 1974, Stephen decided to work over his equations once more. He looked at quantum theory. One of its rules said that, while most people think empty space holds nothing at all, not even energy, a vacuum actually contains energy in the form of particles such as electrons (carrying negative charges) and antiparticles such as positrons (with positive charges). These react with each other, constantly being created and reacting to knock each other out so that the vacuum is a churning ocean of energy. Hawking concluded that the process releases energy from the black hole into the vast universe. This radiation produces greater and greater heat until the hole explodes with gamma rays and X rays.

Scientists knew that the wavelengths of X rays are much shorter than the wavelengths of light, while radio wavelengths are much longer. That means that light waves and radio waves can get through the Earth's atmosphere but X rays cannot (luckily for us, for the human race could not survive large-scale exposure to X rays). So they had no way to observe space X rays from Earth. But newly invented satellites in orbit outside the Earth's atmosphere could detect them, and did.

Satellites checking for X rays found a source of them that was between eight and 10 times the size of our sun. Naming it Cygnus X-1, the observers felt 95 percent sure that it was the first black hole ever identified. The finding of Cygnus X-1 would eventually prove that Stephen Hawking had led one of history's most significant works in scientific research. He had put together three concepts: the quantum theory of physics (which dealt with the tiniest of the tiny particles that make up all matter), the general theory of relativity (which dealt with the relative movement of all matter in space), and the basic theory of thermodynamics (which dealt with the behavior of heat and cold).

One of Stephen's friends put it more simply. Upon learning that Hawking had figured out that black holes not only emit radiation but can actually explode, he greeted

Dr. Sciama with the words, "Have you heard? Stephen's changed everything!"

In *Nature* magazine, scientists soon read Stephen's own paper describing how radiation was emitted by black holes. They began calling the phenomenon Hawking Radiation.

Party Animal Wins Awards

Even though he was making so much progress in his work, Stephen was by no means confined to his offices at the Institute of Astronomy and at the DAMTP. His reputation was growing worldwide. Invitations to speak at conferences and seminars came frequently, even though someone had to read his papers to the audience for him. In fact, he could no longer write in longhand or use a typewriter. Nevertheless, he did not hesitate to accept opportunities to appear all over the world.

Stephen's wheelchair did not keep him from having fun. He and Jane loved to dance, and they did so at parties from Cambridge to New York City. A big fan of rock and roll, in particular the group the Beatles, Stephen was able to move in rhythm, spinning his wheelchair around the dance floor in time with the music. The robust energy he took to his work also went into his play. One close friend who enjoyed watching Stephen and Jane dance in New York called him a "real party animal."

More and more, the world was taking notice of Stephen Hawking. Black holes were in the news. Television documentaries about them were being produced. In March 1974, soon after the announcement of Hawking Radiation, the Royal Society invited Stephen to become a fellow. This was Britain's highest academic honor—one of the highest honors any scientist could dream of. At only 32, Stephen was one of the youngest recipients of this honor in the history of the society. At the ceremony for new fellows, each was expected to step up to the podium, sign the roll of honor, and shake the hand of the president. But when Hawking's turn came, the president, Sir Alan Hodgkin, a Nobel-prize-winning biophysicist, picked up the roll and carried it down to Stephen in the front row. While everyone in the hall waited spellbound in silence, Stephen painstakingly signed his name—one letter at a time. Then, as Hodgkin lifted the book from Stephen's lap, roaring applause burst forth.

Caltech, Sunshine, and Curb Ramps

In the summer of 1974, Jane Hawking had to pack up books, clothing, and belongings for herself, her two young children, and her nearly helpless husband. She lined up schedules and booked airline tickets. The family was off to the California Institute of Technology (better known as Caltech) in Pasadena, a suburb of Los Angeles, for a year.

Stephen had been invited there, on a Sherman Fairchild Distinguished Scholarship, to do research in cosmology with a prominent physicist named Kip Thorne.

Caltech was quite small, with only about 1,500 students. But it was a world leader in science and technology, boasting Nobel Prize winners and earning major contributions from such corporations as IBM and Wang. Kip Thorne, who wore his gray hair shoulder-length and dressed in beads and floral shirts, was its leader in theories on relativity. He and Don Page, a graduate student with whom Stephen soon wrote a paper on black holes, became life-long friends of the Hawkings. And Caltech itself helped Stephen in a way that Cambridge never had: Near Stephen's office, the school built ramps to get his wheelchair over the curbs, and it provided him with an up-to-date office that included all the supporting equipment he needed for his research.

During the year, Stephen concentrated on black holes. By December he had worked out equations that used the general theory of relativity to prove that a black hole's surface area could not shrink. He set out to apply quantum rules to his equations. This was no easy task. Even Einstein had never been able to unite quantum theory (that is, the theory that energy such as light is absorbed or produced in tiny units called quanta or photons that move in waves) and relativity theory (that is, the theory that mass can be changed into energy) into a single theory. What Stephen was now trying to figure out was what happens when a dying black hole evaporates.

Back in England in the summer of 1975, Stephen and Jane realized that their tiny home was now just too tiny for the family. As Stephen's body deteriorated, his struggle up and down the stairs had become an almost impossible challenge. They asked the university, which had never before responded to their needs, to help them find a suitable home. It answered, to their surprise, with an apartment on the ground floor of a large Victorian house it owned only 10 minutes by wheelchair from Stephen's DAMTP office. Behind the house, a large garden and lawn area were maintained by university gardeners.

During the year in California, Jane had become Stephen's round-the-clock nurse, for he had more and more difficulty feeding himself and getting in and out of bed. To help relieve her of some of the load, and because their new home had an extra room, they invited one of Stephen's graduate students to become student-in-residence. He earned free lodging in exchange for such duties as babysitting, handling general household repairs, and lining up lecture dates and travel arrangements. One of the first of many such students later said that living with the Hawkings was "like participating in history."

Playing Tag, Winning Awards

Stephen could no longer drive his three-wheeled car. Instead, he now sat slumped in an electric wheelchair he could control by pushing buttons with his fingertips. It gave him more independence, for he no longer needed to have someone meet his car and help him into his manual wheelchair. Even better, he could roll speedily around his backyard, playing tag with his children.

He was also speeding into international fame. He received six major awards in 1975 and 1976, including The Royal Astronomical Society's Eddington Medal and the Pius XI Medal from the Pontifical Academy of Science at the Vatican. In the winter of 1976, he returned to the United States for major conferences in Chicago and Boston.

While event planners always knew Hawking would arrive in his wheelchair, none provided ramps or lifting devices to get it onto the stage. Instead, at the last minute they usually enlisted the five or six of the strongest scientists present to heave the wheelchair (which was loaded with hefty automobile batteries) and its occupant (who weighed barely 90 pounds) up stairs and onto platforms.

In January 1977, British television viewers by the millions watched a BBC program called *The Key to the Universe*. It gave the general public its first chance to understand Stephen Hawking's attempts to put quantum mechanics and general relativity together. It also let the public in on the facts about how a man could be diagnosed with ALS at 21 and live to be a world-famous scientist at 35. The TV program brought Stephen worldwide publicity. Cambridge University, embarrassed as questioners wondered why this celebrated physicist had not been made a professor, created a special Chair of Gravitational Physics for him and made him a professorial fellow at Caius. Oxford University, realizing that Cambridge was getting so much credit for the achievements of one of Oxford's graduates, got in on the publicity by making Stephen an honorary fellow.

While Stephen was winning the honors, Jane was doing all the work of keeping house and raising their children. Stephen's duties at home consisted mainly of playing what games he could with the children (chess was one). He gave Jane full credit not only for home-making but for all she had done, and was doing, to help his success. Nevertheless, Jane often found herself feeling like a fifth wheel or unrecognized extra at official gatherings where her husband was the center of attention. "Sometimes I'm not even introduced to people," she once said. "I come along behind and I don't really know who I'm speaking to."

To help herself break out of such hampered feelings, Jane went to work specializing in Portuguese and Spanish poetry in a course in medieval languages that would earn her a Ph.D. It would make it possible for her to become a schoolteacher in Cambridge.

In 1978, Stephen received one of the very highest awards in physics: the Albert Einstein Award of the Lewis and Rose Strauss Memorial Fund. He traveled to Washington, D.C., to accept it, knowing that many scientists considered it equal to a Nobel Prize. Journalists and commentators expressed their views, saying Dr. Hawking should indeed win the Nobel. Others pointed out that Nobel Prizes went to scientists whose discoveries could be proved by verified experiments or by evidence that others could observe. No theory proposed by Stephen had yet been proved. No black hole had yet actually been found. No Hawking Radiation had yet shown up on any testing device.

6

IN NEWTON'S FOOTSTEPS

By the spring of 1979, Stephen Hawking was popularly called "the new Einstein." Jane officially became Dr. Hawking, for she had completed her Ph.D. And on April 15, she delivered the Hawkings' third child, Timothy Stephen Hawking. Despite his new child and busy schedule, Stephen Hawking could do almost nothing for himself except think. He could not feed himself. He needed nursing care around the clock. And England's National Health Service provided only meager help.

Growing Recognition

Now Cambridge University recognized Stephen in two ways. First, its press published a book co-edited by him that contained 16 articles commemorating the 100th anniversary of Einstein's birth on March 14, 1879. Titled

The Hawkings and their children in 1980 (Time Life Pictures/Getty Images)

General Relativity: An Einstein Centenary Survey, it became an instant best-seller.

Second, the university appointed Stephen as Lucasian Professor of Mathematics, a title to which Isaac Newton had been appointed 310 years earlier. At the ceremony installing him, the new professor sat onstage, slumped and unable to move in his wheelchair, as his unforgettable lecture "Is the End in Sight for Theoretical Physics?" was read for him. It proposed that a "Grand Unified Theory" that described the fundamental laws of the universe might be realized by the end of the 20th century. It also offered his prediction about computers, which were then developing rapidly into household and business necessities. "It would seem quite possible," he said, "that they will take over altogether in theoretical physics." Then, astonishing his devoted audience, he closed with the remark, "Maybe the end is in sight for theoretical physicists, if not for theoretical physics."

Champion for the Disabled

For several years Stephen had been fighting to get various authorities to recognize the needs of the disabled. It had taken years for him to convince the university that it should pay for a ramp in the DAMTP building, where, upon his appointment as Lucasian Professor, he at last had a private office. He had also finally persuaded them to lower the curbs along his route from home to office. Then he had tackled the Cambridge City Council because, during elections, disabled voters found no ramps giving them access to polling places. He won that one, too.

Such efforts brought him a different kind of recognition. Late in 1979, the Royal Association for Disability and Rehabilitation made him its Man of the Year. Friends were pleased, yet all who knew Stephen well were aware that he loved a good fight on any subject, from cosmology to curb ramps, but that he also hated to use his own physical condition as a lever to gain any advantage. They knew that he did not feel that being a disabled celebrity gave him any special right to attention.

When Did Time Begin?

As the 1980s began, Stephen grappled with the question of how quantum mechanics and relativity had blended when time began. Then he wondered: What if time never did begin?

He thought about that fundamental principle of physics that he knew so well: the basic uncertainty principle. No one could be absolutely certain about such basic measures as length and time. And he thought about another principle called Planck's constant (named after Max Planck, a German pioneer in quantum physics). It said that not even the teeniest tiny bit of matter, incredibly smaller than the nucleus of an atom, could be smaller than what physicists called Planck length. No shrinking black hole could get smaller than one Planck length in diameter. Nor could any length of time, not even an infinitesimal fraction of a second, get any shorter than Planck time. There was no moment to point to as the beginning of time.

To help others grasp his complex thinking about space-time, Stephen used a simple analogy. Suppose the universe was a vast globe like the Earth, he suggested, that contained all energy and matter as well as all time and space. And suppose the Big Bang came at a tiny, tightly compacted point precisely at the North Pole of this globe. Everyone knows that from the North Pole, no matter which way you turn, the only direction in space is south. In the same way, from the Big Bang, the only direction in time is toward the future. There is no past, no before or beginning.

Hawking took this theory to Pope John Paul II. In 1981 the Pontifical Academy of Sciences in the Vatican organized a week-long conference on cosmology. There Stephen revealed his latest conclusions on the origin of the universe, which many scientists soon called his *no-boundary theorem*. Following the conference, the pope invited the cosmologists to an audience with him at Castel Gandolfo, his summer residence. Each visitor came forward to be introduced to the pope, knelt before him to chat briefly, and stepped aside. Then Stephen rolled forward in his chair. The guests watched in surprise as the pope rose from his elevated chair on its platform, stepped down, knelt so his face was at the same level as Stephen's, and conversed with him longer than he had with the others. The pope had heard about Stephen's theory that proposed that time had no beginning. The idea that time had no beginning implies that there could have been no creation. Since the creation story is a vital part of the Catholic faith, it was startling to see the pope in earnest conversation with Stephen Hawking.

Stubbornness and Money

Stephen showed his stubborn, insistent side soon after the Vatican trip. Cambridge University Press was preparing his book *Superspace and Supergravity* for publication. The press expected to sell somewhere between 5,000 and 10,000 copies over several years—not a big sale. For the book's cover, Stephen wanted the publishers to use a drawing that was on the blackboard in his office. The drawing was in full color, and Stephen wanted it printed in full color. The publishers said the book would never sell enough copies to justify the cost of full-color printing. The cover would have to be in black and white. Stephen said no, insisting that he would withdraw the book from publication if he couldn't have his way. The press editors gave in, and the book never sold enough copies to pay for its full-color cover.

Honors continued to come Stephen's way. In 1981, Queen Elizabeth II made him a Commander of the British Empire, an appointment that ranks just below a knighthood. The next year, Britain's University of Leicester and Princeton, Notre Dame, and New York Universities in the United States each gave him an honorary doctor of science degree. He made it a point to travel to each ceremony. He

Stephen has received many awards and distinctions throughout his career, including being made a Commander of the British Empire. He is pictured here with England's Queen Mother. (Campix)

liked the fame and attention, and he was still (as he had always been) an avid sightseer and visitor to unfamiliar places.

While he enjoyed all this, Stephen's sharp mind kept turning over a problem that dealt not with the vastness of space but with an acute problem in his household and family: money. The Hawkings did not have enough of it. For a family of five, a professor's salary was barely enough if there were no extraordinary expenses. But, more and more, Jane needed private nursing help to care for Stephen, and now Robert was going to a private school and would soon be in college. Lucy was ready to enter private school, and little Timothy was racing along toward his first school days. The family needed money for tuition and school expenses.

Sitting unmoving in his electric wheelchair, Stephen developed an idea that might solve his family's financial problems.

7

CREATING A BEST-SELLER

Ever since Stephen joined the Institute of Astronomy in 1970, its administrative director, Simon Mitton, had been urging him to write a book about cosmology for the general public. Stephen had never been interested. But late in 1982, he began mulling over the idea.

Stephen knew that writing such a book would steal time from his important research work. Because of his physical condition, writing would be a slow and tedious process. But if the book sold well, it could help solve his financial problems. He wrote a sample chapter and got in touch with Mitton.

Mitton himself had written popular books about science. He knew what might sell and what probably would not sell. He read Stephen's sample chapter and told him it was much too technical. "It's like baked beans," he said. "The blander the flavor, the broader the market. There simply isn't a commercial niche for specialist books like this, Stephen."

Stephen revised the chapter. In January 1983 Mitton reviewed it. "It's still far too technical," he reported. "Look at it this way, Steve—every equation will halve your sales."

Stephen asked him to explain. "When people look at a book in a shop," said Mitton, "they just flick through it to decide if they want to read it. You've got equations on practically every page. When they look at this, they'll say, 'This book's got sums in it,' and put it back on the shelf."

Once Stephen began to write for a general readership, he and Mitton talked about money. Stephen insisted on an advance payment that was larger than Cambridge University Press (the candidate for publisher of the book) had ever provided any author. Mitton went off to negotiate with the press. Next day, he sent Stephen a contract that met his demands.

At almost the same time as Stephen was meeting with Simon Mitton, a man on the other side of the Atlantic Ocean named Peter Guzzardi was reading the article "The Universe and Dr. Hawking" in the *New York Times Magazine*. Guzzardi was a senior editor at Bantam Books in New York. He was intrigued by the story of a man who had not only lived with ALS for 20 years but revolutionized scientists' thinking about the cosmos. He told authors' agent Al Zuckerman that, from what he read in the magazine article, he was sure that Hawking could write a popular book about cosmology. Zuckerman agreed. He too had seen the article. He got in touch with Stephen Hawking.

A $250,000 Advance

Stephen set aside the proposed contract from Cambridge University Press. Over the next six months, he produced 100 pages of sample text and a proposal outlining his book. Zuckerman distributed them to various publishers and held an auction by telephone to give them a chance to bid for the book. Bantam Books, led by Guzzardi, won by offering a $250,000 advance and agreeing to pay top-notch royalties (that is, payments of a percentage of the price of each book sold). Now Stephen faced the challenge of putting his theory on the origin and development of the universe into words and sentences that the everyday reader could understand.

In the meantime, Hawking's reputation kept growing. In 1983, the BBC's *Horizon* program was praised for a program about Stephen. It showed his home life with Jane, Robert, Lucy, and Timothy. The cameras also followed his daily schedule of buzzing along Cambridge streets in his wheelchair and conversing with students and professors in what seemed to viewers to be, with

Stephen's distorted speech, a foreign language. Stephen's friends noted how much he enjoyed the attention and fame.

While Stephen was dividing his time between his book and his continuing research, he and other physicists began rethinking their ideas about such things as electrons and *quarks,* which they had thought of as points—like extremely tiny dots. Quarks, first predicted by American physicist Murray Gell-Mann (who won a 1969 Nobel Prize for his discovery), are even smaller than subatomic particles and are considered to be a part of protons and neutrons (which themselves make up nuclear particles). Maybe, thought the physicists, such particles were not points but had length and were like strings. They called their thinking *string theory.* The strings were so very, very tiny that it would take many of them, end to end, to reach across the diameter of a proton. Some might be closed, like tiny loops. Others might be open, their ends flapping freely. None, the scientists agreed, had any dimension except length.

For a year and a half, Stephen worked on writing his book, sending one section after another to editor Guzzardi in New York. Back came two pages of comment for every page of text, for Guzzardi was determined to see that his author wrote a readable, understandable book. "I was persistent," Guzzardi later said, "and kept on until

Hawking made me understand things. He may have thought I was a little thick, but I risked it and kept on plugging away until I saw what he was talking about."

Even before he completed his first draft of text, Stephen accepted an invitation in 1984 to tour China and lecture in several cities. Standing-room-only audiences greeted him, and, always the eager sightseer, he found time to drive his wheelchair along the Great Wall.

The early summer of 1985 saw him on a world lecture tour. In Chicago, a large crowd of world physicists at Fermilab (a high-energy physicists research organization) watched aghast as one of them had to pick Stephen up in his arms and carry him through the audience and onto the stage while another fetched the wheelchair. Next day, for a public lecture, people were turned away from an overcrowded auditorium. Those inside were amazed to hear Hawking, speaking on "The Direction of Time," say that some day in the far-off future the universe could be expected to collapse back to a singularity. When that occurred, Stephen predicted, time would also turn back and everything that ever happened would happen again— backward.

A Health Scare

By July 1985, Stephen was in Geneva, Switzerland, working at CERN (European Center for Nuclear Research) headquarters and rewriting some sections of his book to meet his editor's recommendations. With a full-time nurse and a research assistant, Stephen lived in a rented apartment while Jane toured Germany visiting old friends. One night early in August, the nurse found him gasping and turning purple.

Doctors discovered a blockage in Stephen's windpipe and suspected he had pneumonia, which is often fatal to ALS victims. They hooked him up to a ventilator to give him automatic breathing.

After two weeks, an air ambulance flew Stephen back to Cambridge. With their patient still on the ventilator, the doctors told Jane his only hope for survival was a tracheostomy—an operation in which a breathing gadget is inserted through the neck and into the windpipe just above the collarbone. This would save his life but would mean he could never again make any sound with his voice. Jane agreed. After the surgery, her husband spent several more weeks in the hospital.

In the meantime, seeking financial help, Jane wrote to charitable organizations worldwide. The Hawkings' old friends Kip Thorne and particle physicist Murray Gell-Mann helped her with recommendations to the John and Catherine MacArthur Foundation, which agreed to pay a major share of the cost of Stephen's day-and-night nursing at home.

A New Voice

On November 4, 1985, Stephen returned home from the hospital. But he could not make even the badly slurred speech that those who knew him were used to. Then came stirring news. A California computer expert named Walt Woltosz had written a program called Equalizer. He sent it to Stephen. Using a small mouse that he could manage to control, Stephen could select any of some 3,000 words onscreen and line them up as sentences. Some basic sentences, in fact, were already included in the program. Stephen could then send his onscreen words and sentences to a voice synthesizer that turned them into clear, understandable sounds.

The husband of one of Stephen's nurses was a talented computer engineer. He adapted the synthesizer and computer to Stephen's wheelchair. Now the world's foremost cosmologist could not only be understood when he lectured or conversed; he could take his new voice with him anywhere. It had only two problems. It spoke with an American, not British, accent, and it took time to assemble the sentences. "But then I think slowly," said Stephen, "so it suited me quite well." And he got a kick out of opening lectures and conversations with a sentence he created and saved: "Hello, please excuse my American accent."

A year after Stephen Hawking had been found gasping and purple-hued, he was back in form, traveling widely to

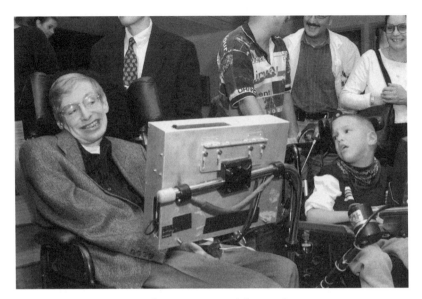

Stephen uses a special computer with a voice program to communicate with others. Here he visits a young patient at Children's Hospital in Boston. (Associated Press)

give lectures and attend conferences. With his computer speaking for him, he no longer needed a human interpreter. In December 1986 a Chicago audience was pleased to hear him take back the astounding idea he had expressed there a year earlier. He was now convinced, he said, that time would not go backward when the universe ultimately condensed.

During 1987, Stephen proofread the pages of his book, making changes and corrections. At the same time, he kept in touch with his agent, Al Zuckerman, who was lining up publishers in Italy, Spain, France, Germany, Japan, Korea,

China, the Scandinavian countries, and Russia. Yet no publisher in the United Kingdom was ready to make a deal for this promising book by Britain's world-famous cosmologist.

Finally, the director of Bantam UK, Mark Barty-King, reluctantly agreed to publish the book throughout the United Kingdom. He was not sure he had made the right decision until, in the fall of 1987, he met Stephen Hawking at the Frankfurt Book Fair, a major international publishing event held in Germany. "It's only when you meet him," Barty-King said afterward, "that you realize how extraordinary he is. What in particular comes as such a surprise, after all he has been through, is that you get such a strong impression of his sense of humour."

"A book by one of the greatest minds"

Publishers who gathered to hear Stephen speak in Frankfurt were charmed as he reported on his life and career and reasons for writing such a book. And speaking of the book itself, Barty-King said, "It's a book by one of the greatest minds of our time, discussing the elemental subject of who we are and where we come from. It is a lucid and very personal book, one which I personally found quite difficult to read because of the subject-matter, but one which I considered to have enormous appeal."

Reviewing final page proofs, Stephen worried about the proposed title *A Brief History of Time*. He thought maybe *brief* was too flippant a word. Guzzardi said it was just the right word, for it made him smile. "Stephen saw the point immediately," said Guzzardi. "He likes to make people smile."

Stephen was in New York for the book's launch party early in the spring of 1988. There, after a day of meetings and celebrations, he made an enthusiastic speech about his book. The party lasted until well after midnight, with Stephen's whirling, dancing wheelchair leading the fun.

Only a few days later, a Bantam editor noticed that two illustrations in the book were misplaced. Bantam sales staff was ordered to phone the major bookstores and chains and recall the 40,000 copies distributed from the first print run. They were astonished to find they couldn't get any back. All had been sold, and orders for more were pouring in.

By midsummer 1988, the corrected *A Brief History of Time* was on all best-seller lists and had sold more than a half-million copies in the United States. What pleased Stephen the most was that his book could be bought from bookracks in every airport in the United States.

Published in England in June 1988, the book sold out its first print run on the first day of sale and went on to enjoy 234 weeks on the best-seller list. More than 600,000 hardcover books were bought before Bantam UK issued the paperback edition.

The Hawking family, led by a husband and father who could not move or speak and who could barely lift a finger, began to realize that with the publication of this worldwide best-seller they could breathe a little more easily.

8

MOVING AT FULL THROTTLE

With *A Brief History of Time* in the hands of millions of readers worldwide, life changed not only in the Hawking family but at the DAMTP in Cambridge. Over the next couple of years, television crews came and went, producing one documentary or news feature after another. In the United States, the ABC television program *20/20* produced a feature on Hawking. At King's College in London, the admissions office saw applications for the study of mathematics increase substantially, thanks to young students' interest in Stephen Hawking. Journalists arrived for interviews and noted countless details of the rundown office that Cambridge University provided for the world's foremost cosmologist, including, to their surprise, a giant Marilyn Monroe poster mounted on the back of his office door.

On July 3, 1988, a visiting reporter from the *San Antonio Express News* in Texas gave his readers this description of the Hawking he saw:

> He hurtles out into the street. At full throttle the chair is capable of a decent trotting pace, and Hawking likes to use full throttle. He also knows no fear. He simply shoots out into the middle of the road on the assumption that any passing cars will stop. His assistants rush nervously out ahead of him to try to minimize the danger.

Stephen's daredevil wheelchair driving nearly led to disaster on one occasion. In June 1989 he visited Oxford University to deliver the famed Halley Lecture (named for the discoverer of the seen-once-in-a-lifetime comet). A young physics professor named George Efstathiou was appointed to escort Stephen to the theater. This meant riding in an elevator so small it could hold only two people. Several feet from the elevator's open door, Efstathiou was astonished to see Stephen push his wheelchair button for full-speed-ahead. His wheelchair rushed pell-mell into the elevator. There he stopped, his chair awkwardly jammed and his back to the door, which closed with one wheel blocking it slightly open. Frantic, Efstathiou managed to squeeze an arm through the narrow gap. He could just reach the *open door* button. Out came a grinning Hawking at full-speed-astern.

Letters to Answer, Celebrities to Meet

Stephen was now receiving more invitations to speak in public than he could possibly accept. He needed a research assistant and a secretary to handle the daily volume of mail. They created a *cranks file*, which held often amusing letters from amateur scientists who thought they had answers to questions about the universe. They also fielded numbers of harsh letters from religious zealots who thought that physicists were intruding into God's realm.

The religion question was put directly to Stephen in December 1988, when he was invited to a dinner party with actress Shirley MacLaine. MacLaine was known as a student of metaphysics, a field of philosophy concerned not only with cosmology but with the nature of all existence. For years, she had consulted with teachers and holy men about the meaning of the universe and of all life. Now, at the dinner table, she asked Stephen Hawking whether he believed in a God who created the universe. After a moment, his voice synthesizer spoke one word: "No."

In 1989 England's Queen Elizabeth II, at a special ceremony presided over by her husband, Prince Philip, included Stephen Hawking on her Honors List for the second time, appointing him a Companion of Honor. Also that year, Cambridge University, despite the fact that a university almost never awards an honorary doctorate to its own employees, made Stephen an honorary Doctor of Science and produced a special concert in his honor. There Stephen rolled onstage to thank the audience and musicians, who had just played his favorite Wagner piece, *Ride of the Valkyries*. Describing the standing ovation Stephen received, a journalist wrote, "There were tears rolling down the cheeks of men and women as a tribute to his courage, as well as the exceptional brain that has continued to advance knowledge of time and space in spite of the ravages of a crippling disease."

Stephen's positive, aggressive attitude about his own disability showed clearly in a speech he made at the University of Southern California in 1989. Addressing a conference of scientists through his voice synthesizer, he said:

> It is very important that disabled children should be helped to blend with others of the same age. It determines their self-image. How can one feel a member of the human race if one is set apart from an early age? It is a form of apartheid. Aids like wheelchairs

and computers can play an important role in overcoming physical deficiencies; the right attitude is even more important. It is no use complaining about the public's attitude about the disabled. It is up to disabled people to change people's awareness in the same way that blacks and women have changed public perceptions.

In Cambridge that year, Stephen helped create a special hostel for handicapped students in memory of Bridget Spufford. The disabled daughter of a Cambridge professor, Spufford had not been able to find any English university that could handle her needs. Stephen helped lead a campaign to raise nearly $1 million. He described his own experience with the university's utter lack of interest in providing ramps until it was forced to and pointed out that it had ignored an act of Parliament dating from 1970 that ordered institutions to provide access to the disabled.

At Bristol University, Stephen helped raise the money to build a dormitory for handicapped students. In his honor, it was named Hawking House.

In the Movies

The Hawking family no longer suffered from a shortage of money. Royalties from the sale of millions of copies of *A Brief History of Time* now paid for the day-and-night

Stephen with president of Microsoft Inc., Bill Gates
(Associated Press)

nursing Stephen needed and for his children's education. In addition, the book's success brought Stephen a
new project.

A former ABC news producer named Gordon Freedman had bought the book's film rights. He went to Steven
Spielberg, the famous Hollywood filmmaker, who got NBC
interested and proposed as director Errol Morris, writer-
director of the much-admired film *The Thin Blue Line*.
Freedman next offered the project to Britain's Anglia Television. Then a deal was made with Tokyo Broadcasting, so
production costs would be split among American, English,
and Japanese backing.

Stephen was especially pleased to learn that Spielberg
was interested in his story. They met in Los Angeles early
in 1990 and talked about two of Hawking's favorite
movies, *E.T.* and *Close Encounters of the Third Kind*.

Director Morris came up with a script approach quite
different from the text in the book, building it around a
series of more than 30 interviews. In Anglia Television's
Elstree studios, 33 different sets were built. One repro-
duced Hawking's childhood home. Another re-created his
office at the DAMTP, complete with the Marilyn Monroe
poster. When Morris asked Stephen about that, he learned
that *Some Like It Hot* was the cosmologist's favorite movie
and that his wife and children had long teased him by giving him Monroe posters, towels, and bags.

Stephen spent long hours in the studio. In his wheelchair, parked under the bright lights, he earned the admiration of the film crew as he performed in front of a blue screen. This enabled technicians later to project his image against any needed background. "I can place Stephen Hawking where he belongs," said Morris, "in a mental landscape rather than a real one." The result was an intriguing series of special effects that helped translate Stephen's words into the medium of film.

End of the Marriage

In the summer of 1990, after being married for 25 years, Jane and Stephen separated. Close friends knew that, after years of devoting all her time to Stephen's needs, Jane was now able to find time for her own work and her interests in reading, gardening, and singing in Cambridge's finest choir. They also knew that Jane was a deeply religious person who had gained from her faith much of the strength she needed to cope with her husband's disability. Stephen, on the other hand, had become more and more convinced that the universe he knew so well had no place for God. The greatly admired couple apparently had agreed to disagree.

Stephen moved into an apartment with Elaine Mason, who had been his nurse for several years and whose former husband had enabled Stephen's mini-computer and voice synthesizer to work from his wheelchair. Twenty-three-year-old Robert Hawking, who was now a Cambridge graduate student in physics, and 20-year-old Lucy, an Oxford student in modern languages, were old enough to accept their parents' breakup. For 11-year-old Timothy, however, it was hard to understand.

Hoping to offer TV viewers and tabloid readers a juicy story about the world-famous celebrity physicist's private life, journalists besieged the Hawking home and pestered neighbors for information and quotable remarks. The Hawkings' friends said nothing. Stephen himself made it a rule that no interview could include questions about his personal life.

Some friends felt that Stephen showed signs of depression following the separation. The twinkle in his eye (for years almost his only means of facial expression) seemed to have diminished. Others thought his spirits were as light as ever. One example of spirit came in December 1990 when he appeared for a lecture in the giant Brighton Conference Center. The building included several auditoriums. In one next door to where Stephen was to speak, the rock group Status Quo was appearing. Tickets for them had been sold out for months.

At 8:30 on the night before his talk, Stephen was expected in a meeting in his hotel room. He did not show up. Friends and journalists awaiting him found out that Stephen's students, knowing how much he wanted to see and hear Status

Quo, had managed to get him complimentary tickets simply by mentioning to the Status Quo managers that a fan named Stephen Hawking was in the building.

Time Travel?

As the 1990s unfolded, Stephen was wondering about time travel. After all, physicists had known for years that Einstein's general theory of relativity described not merely space but spacetime. They had long thought that maybe there could be such a thing as a natural time machine. Suppose, they thought, that matter collapsing into a black hole—that is, toward a singularity—could be moving kind of sideways in spacetime. It would turn into a new universe, expanding within its own group of spacetime dimensions. Yet it would still be connected, by a sort of tunnel, to the original black hole. The scientists called this tunnel, which they described as a shortcut through spacetime, a *wormhole*. For years, the idea had given science-fiction writers inspiration for all kinds of stories in which spaceships almost instantly moved from one galaxy to another or across the vastness of any universe.

Stephen figured out that before any wormhole could begin operating as a time machine its buildup of electromagnetic energy would produce radiation inside it—very much like Hawking Radiation—that would destroy it. In effect, he said, time travel was impossible.

9

TV STAR AND NEW MARRIAGE

Everyday travel in his wheelchair gave Stephen, one of his nurses, and all his friends a real scare in the spring of 1991. Headed home after dark with his nurse, he was rolling along at full speed when he came to an intersection. A speeding taxi driver did not see him. The taxi smashed the wheelchair, destroying it, damaging Stephen's computer, throwing him to the pavement, breaking his shoulder, and slashing his face. He spent only two days in the hospital before he was back at work in his office.

One Book for Every 970 People

Editing the film *A Brief History of Time* was so complex that it was not released in theaters in Europe and America until the spring of 1992, when it met with good reviews. Some critics pointed out that the film seemed to have too much biography and not enough science. Stephen himself admitted that he had been concerned about that aspect of the film, but he had been assured by its producers that including details about his life would bring people in to see the movie. To producer David Hickman, the film was neither the biography of a disabled physicist nor a documentary about science. Rather, he thought of it as a very special film dealing with religion and time. "The most exciting thing about cosmology," he remarked, "is the fact that it interfaces metaphysics and conventional science."

The book on which the film was based had now been translated into 30 languages. Five and a half million copies had been sold. As Stephen the mathematician pointed out, that was the equivalent of one book for every 970 human beings worldwide.

Neither he nor anyone else could be quite sure what made the book so popular. Some critics said people bought the book not to read but just so they could say they had it. Others thought that probably many copies were bought because the buyers admired Stephen's courage. After all, he had overcome a severe, ever-growing handicap. He had led as normal a life as possible despite his illness. And he had achieved world-wide success and fame.

Stephen's mother answered the question of the book's popularity probably better than anyone else did. She responded to a request published by the *Independent*, a British magazine, for readers' opinions on why the Hawking book was so well liked. She said it was because it was so well written. "The ideas are difficult," she said, "not the language." She added that anyone who was interested in her son's ideas could understand them.

A Busy Writer and Media Figure

Stephen's days now seemed occupied less with cosmology and more with writing and publishing. He knew that he could build both his income and his reputation on the basis of his best-seller. In 1992 he published *A Companion to A Brief History of Time*, a book that gave readers the behind-the-scenes story of the film. On Christmas Day that year, he was heard (by way of his voice synthesizer) on *Desert Island Discs*, a program of England's Radio 4. During the broadcast, Stephen described how he had handled his ALS and introduced his favorite selections from the music of Wagner, Brahms, Beethoven, and the Beatles.

Stephen's next book was *Black Holes and Baby Universes*, a 1993 collection of 13 of his essays. They included self-portraits of his family and personal life, comments on religion, and lectures on up-to-date technology.

That spring Hawking began appearing in television commercials for British Telecom, the national telephone company known as BT. His 90-second messages told viewers about the importance of communication. Everything in history, he said, had been accomplished through people talking.

BT paid Stephen well for the TV work. He enjoyed it just as he had enjoyed making the film version of *A Brief History of Time*. Later in 1993 he visited the studio where *Star Trek: The Next Generation* was being videotaped. He mentioned to the producers that he had always wished he could appear on the program. They wrote a part for him in an episode in which he played poker aboard the starship *Enterprise* with Albert Einstein, Sir Isaac Newton, and Data (a character from the show). He began to think about the possibility of having his own TV show.

"God still has a few tricks up his sleeve."

Stephen used his growing fame to try to help others. He lent his name to charities that worked at national and local levels to help the physically disabled. For example, to attract media and public attention to a Science Museum exhibition of future technology that would help the disabled, he appeared in person as the official ribbon-cutter. In a March 1994 letter to *The Times*, he criticized the establishment for not understanding that the disabled "face great obstacles when they want to take part in any normal activities like going to the theatre or cinema, or eating in restaurants. As I know only too well, very few London theatres and cinemas have wheelchair places."

Not everyone agreed on the value of Stephen's fame. Some critics thought he was arrogant—that is, conceited and egotistical—in the way he claimed that physical science had all the answers and religion had none. Yet they admitted that he was the scientific genius of the late 20th century and that, when Stephen Hawking spoke on any subject, the world listened.

The world was listening in the summer of 1995 when Stephen lectured at the 5,000-seat Royal Albert Hall. The event drew the largest crowd England had seen for a physics lecture since Albert Einstein's appearance in 1933, with every seat sold and scalpers in the street selling some tickets at high prices. Hawking baffled his critics by ending the talk with comments on God's work in maintaining the universe. "God," he said finally, "still has a few tricks up his sleeve."

Many who had been perplexed by what critics called Stephen's lack of religion liked this concluding remark. It fit well with the ending of *A Brief History of Time*, in which Stephen wrote about the importance of seeking and finding a theory about our universe that unifies quantum physics and general relativity. "If we do discover a complete

theory," his book ends, "it would be the ultimate tri-
umph of human reason—for then we would know the
mind of God."

The "Einstein Wedding"

When Stephen announced, at the Aspen music festival,
his and Elaine Mason's plans to be married, large numbers
of world-famous physicists were present, for Aspen is one
of their favorite meeting places. So it was almost as if he
were talking to family when he used his appearance
onstage to announce the forthcoming wedding. His

*Stephen and his second wife, Elaine; the media dubbed their
wedding ceremony the "Einstein Wedding."* (Campix)

friends sensed his self-confidence and admired his determination—the same insistence with which he had not
only produced his immensely successful book but had
made the most of the publicity it brought him.

Television and news reports of the wedding treated
the couple to the kind of bashing so often given celebri-
ties' remarriages. "Einstein Wedding" was one tabloid
headline. Another said, "Genius Weds Nurse." An interview with Stephen's mother, Isobel Hawking, however,
quoted her sensible point of view: "The coverage of the
wedding and the barrage beforehand were thoroughly
unpleasant. The impression was that Elaine was an
interloper—and she is not. There is nothing disreputable
about the wedding, as the press suggested. It is quite
normal for people who have been together for four years
to get married."

Keeping up with opportunities for publicity and publication gave the newlyweds a busy life. As an international
celebrity, Stephen was now a sort of one-man industry. In
1996 he produced *The Illustrated Brief History of Time,*
which was more readable than the original. It became
another best-seller.

Stephen's television presence grew in 1997 when
another series, *Stephen Hawking's Universe,* was
launched. Now more Britons knew him from television
than from his best-selling *A Brief History of Time.* His

fame as a leading cosmologist stood in a poor third place compared to his renown as a TV personality and as an author.

Hawking's thinking and influence stretched in yet another direction in 1997 when the city of Cambridge got into extensive discussions with Bill Gates and his Microsoft computer company about locating a giant research center there. In the complex negotiations, Stephen represented Cambridge University. The related company, Intel, was so impressed with his haggling skills that it updated his wheelchair software. Now, using a wireless Global System for Mobile communications (GSM), he could connect to the Internet from almost anywhere in the world. The system also enabled him to transmit radio signals to turn on lights, open doors, and operate other electrical equipment by remote control. At the same time, his new laptop sped up the synthesis software that translated his word text to voice. "I have immediate access to the Internet and email wherever I am," he commented.

Early in 1999, on the invitation of President Bill Clinton, Stephen visited the White House. There, as part of the president's *Millennium Evenings* series, he delivered a lecture on various aspects of space and time in the 21st century.

10

HERE, THERE, AND EVERYWHERE

As the 20th century ended, Stephen Hawking was so well known that his opinion was sought on almost any subject. He even expressed his opinions on American politics, watching candidates Al Gore and George W. Bush as they campaigned in the 2000 presidential election. Stephen favored Al Gore, saying that, "The next president of the United States is more than a leader of your country. He will have to pilot the whole world through a period of ever-increasing change brought about by the advances in science and technology that are transforming our lives. Al Gore understands the implications of this change and will be able to shape it and seize its opportunities."

The Universe in a Nutshell

The year 2000 was one of extensive travel for Stephen Hawking. In January he was off to his familiar campus at Caltech in California, where he discussed string theory in a meeting of physicists called the Millennium Conference. The general public got a chance to see and hear him on January 21st in a lecture he titled "The Millennium: Looking Back to See Ahead." By the end of May he was back at Caltech to celebrate his longtime friend Kip Thorne's 60th birthday by lecturing in what the fun-loving physicists called the KipFest Saturday Science Talks.

September took Stephen and his computer-equipped wheelchair to South Korea for several lectures. At the Seoul National University, he spoke before a crowd of 4,000 people; then he moved on to the island of Cheju for the COSMO 2000 conference, which discussed how cosmology and particle physics had interacted in the early universe. By September 29th, he was back on British soil speaking at a large public meeting on behalf of the Royal Society of Edinburgh, Scotland, at the University of Edinburgh.

Constantly preparing for public speeches and traveling around the globe to deliver them gave Stephen a schedule that could exhaust anyone in normal health. To maintain the schedule as well as his lifestyle, he and Elaine employed 10 nurses around the clock. He not only seemed to thrive on his busy agenda and timetable, but also to write and think about the cosmos. During 2000 and early 2001, he was concentrating on a book that would simplify the ideas in *A Brief History of Time* and make them clear to the everyday reader. He called it *The Universe in a Nutshell*.

In Mumbai, India, in January 2001, participants in the international conference *Strings 2001* welcomed Stephen Hawking as a Sarojini Damodaran International Fellow of the Tata Institute of Fundamental Research. Talking with them about science in the future, he covered a variety of related subjects: particle physics, world population, invasion by aliens, and even one of his favorite TV programs, *Star Trek*. As he described advances in science, he reminded his audience that things have changed beyond recognition in the centuries since Aristotle and Galileo and that earthlings must be ready for even greater change in the future.

Stephen also spoke in Delhi before he returned to the United States for six weeks of lectures on the West Coast. There he revealed that the inspiration for his title *The Universe in a Nutshell* had come from Shakespeare, whose Hamlet said, "I could be bounded in a nut shell and count myself king of infinite space." Asking the question so many asked—"Is the universe actually infinite?"—he reviewed developments in cosmology (from Hubble to

The Universe in a Nutshell, *Stephen's second book, was a sequel to his international best-seller* A Brief History of Time. (Associated Press)

Einstein to his own generation of physicists) that have led to the way we view the universe today.

Then it was on to Granada, where Stephen's public lecture was so crowded it had to be projected onto screens in the Science Park nearby to accommodate all the viewers.

The Equivalent of a Ferrari

Early in 2001, Stephen knew he needed a sophisticated wheelchair that could do everything but think. He shopped among various brands designed for people whose physical problems were like his. By March he was driving a chair that could move slowly indoors, maneuver the tight doorways and narrow hallways of London buildings, which weren't designed for wheelchair access, and yet zip across the Cambridge campus and roll easily over rough terrain. The seat provided strong supports to keep his upper body secure. He could alter the pressure in its cushion from soft to firm, and at the touch of a button the chair would raise him to standing position. Its headrest was designed to support him above the neck yet let him enjoy the slight basic movements of shoulders, neck, and head that he still had. And everything could be controlled by a fingertip touching a small laptop device.

"This chair is great," said Stephen as soon as he had taken a test drive. "It's the wheelchair equivalent of a Ferrari. It will make navigating the buildings I use and towns

I visit easier, and so I will be able to spend more time doing what I enjoy." Then, thinking of the chair's top speed of six miles per hour (faster than a walking person in a hurry), he added, "It will also help to keep my nurses fit as they try to keep up."

Stephen's associates grinned. They were even more amused when they discovered the personalized license plate mounted on the chair's rear: T4SWH. Standing for "Tea for Stephen William Hawking," it reminded everyone of the cosmologist's favorite drink.

A New Release

The Universe in a Nutshell came out late that fall. It was a much-anticipated release. Some critics said the book was "the most significant commercial addition" to Stephen's literary works. Others said it was easier to read than *A Brief History of Time* but that it didn't present any new ideas. The book sold well, adding to the Hawking income, but did not match *A Brief History of Time*'s best-selling records.

11

"THE MOST FAMOUS SCIENTIST ALIVE TODAY"

To celebrate Stephen's 60th birthday, on January 8, 2002, more than 200 physicists gathered in Cambridge for a four-day technical scientific workshop to review advances in their field over the past 40 years. They scheduled a full day of lectures open to the public, with Stephen's speech transmitted as a webcast by the BBC. At the same time, he was acclaimed by *+Plus*, an award-winning Web magazine that produced a special edition to honor him.

Commenting on the unusual four-day scientific birthday party, Professor Ian Halliday, who was chief executive officer of the United Kingdom's Particle Physics and Astronomy Research Council (PPARC), said:

Stephen loves to travel and often meets with world leaders to discuss science and technology. Here he is pictured with Chinese President Jiang Zemin (far right) in 2002. (Associated Press)

Not only is Stephen a first-class scientist of global renown who can be guaranteed to stimulate debate amongst his peers, but he is also a world ambassador for science. His achievements have gone far beyond the scientific community. Stephen has brought the excitement of fundamental physics to a truly mass audience, raising the awareness and general knowledge of cosmology and physics to an unprecedented level.

Brane Theory

Later in 2002, Stephen went to Portland, Oregon, where he was greeted by a sold-out crowd of more than 2,800 as he spoke at a conference organized by the Institute for Science Engineering and Public Policy. Here he talked of a "brane new world," a pun on the title of the 1932 book about life in the future called *Brave New World*. Stephen was addressing a subject that more and more physicists were thinking about: They had begun to suspect that the vast universe actually had more dimensions than the four (three of space and one of time) that we all know about. They called this new thinking *brane theory*.

The physicists took the word *brane* from the word *membrane*, which usually means a two-dimensional surface that comes between two three-dimensional volumes of space. The drumhead on a drum, for example, is a membrane that is a two-dimensional piece of material that separates the three-dimensional volume of space inside the drum from the vast three-dimensional volume of space outside it.

The brane theory proposed that our familiar universe, with its four dimensions, may actually function as a membrane between even greater volumes of space that contain more than four, possibly 10 or 11, dimensions of space-time. Within those dimensions, they predicted, the vibrations of one-dimensional strings could create particles of matter. On the surface of a brane, entire universes could exist, and waves of gravity from a neutron star or black hole from the spacetime world on one side of a brane could leak through into a nearby spacetime world on the other side. In Portland's Keller Auditorium, Stephen's talk on this theory, called M-theory by some scientists, held the standing-room-only crowd spellbound.

Back in England at the Science Museum in London on June 25th, 2002, Hawking was presented the Aventis Book Prize for *The Universe in a Nutshell*. This award is one of the most distinguished prizes for nonfiction books and one that salutes the best in popular science. "I didn't expect to win this prize," said Stephen as he accepted it. "After all, my previous book didn't win any prizes, despite selling millions. But I am very pleased to have had better luck this time. Science writing really can have an impact on how we live. Wherever I go all around the world, people want to know more. This has helped raise the profile of science."

The Stephen Hawking Chair

In 2002, Stephen learned that Texans George P. and Cynthia W. Mitchell had given $1 million to establish the Stephen Hawking Chair in Fundamental Physics at Texas A&M University. (In a college, a *chair* is an official position held by a professor that means extra authority or dignity and, usually, extra pay.) The university agreed to match their contribution, making the $2 million Hawking Chair one of the institution's largest.

The first person to earn the Hawking Chair was Texas A&M physics professor Christopher Pope. From 1976 to 1979 he had studied for his Ph.D. under Stephen's guidance at Cambridge, and he had been one of the many graduate students who faithfully lifted the Hawking wheelchair—and Hawking himself—up and down the difficult stairs of the old English buildings. As he learned he had won the chair, Dr. Pope fondly recalled his days with his mentor. "Of course," he said, "he is brimming over with ideas. But he couldn't sit down with paper and pencil himself and do calculations. He would sit and think. He would be a tremendous gold mine of ideas. It was a very, very inspiring experience working with him."

Always eager to try the latest technologies, Stephen agreed in January 2003 to deliver one of his talks as a live audio-visual broadcast, as well as a webcast, from England to several classrooms at the Massachusetts Institute of Technology (MIT). He gave the American students a brief history of particle physics, concentrating on key theories and scientists as far back as Aristotle. Citing long-established theories that "govern most of physics and all of chemistry and biology," he said that, "in principle we should be able to predict human behavior, though I can't say I've had much success myself." The fact is, he added, the human brain contains too many particles for us to do the equations necessary to predict behavior.

Finally, he said that all theories developed to date to explain the universe "are inconsistent or incomplete," and "maybe such a theory isn't possible. Some people will be very disappointed if there is not an ultimate theory. I belong to that camp, but I have changed my mind." He added that we will "always have the challenge of new discovery. Without it, we will stagnate. Long may the search continue."

Nobel Symposium

Stephen went to Sigtuna, Sweden, in August 2003 for a gathering of the world's most distinguished and active scientists. Called the Nobel Symposium on String Theory and Cosmology, the six-day meeting was designed to increase understanding of the extremely small and the extremely large. Bringing together the two subjects—the tiniest of the tiny and the vastness of spacetime that goes on and on—was still a challenge. The scientists talked about the concept of cosmic inflation and how it had answered several tough questions about the initial moment—the Big Bang—yet left unanswered the question, Did time have a beginning? And they discussed the fact that no final theory had yet been accepted for how intense energies and extremely short distances—the key elements of string theory—work. All agreed that the symposium's various sessions showed how cosmology and string theory had been growing closer together in recent years.

Dark Matter and Dark Energy

More than 70 of the world's leading scientists gathered in Cleveland, Ohio, on the weekend of October 11, 2003, to launch the new Center for Education and Research in Cosmology and Astrophysics (CERCA) at Case Western Reserve University. The $25 million center was the brainchild of Lawrence Krauss, Case's leading theoretical physicist, who had long been one of Stephen's friends. In fact, Stephen had written the foreword to a Krauss book, *The Physics of Star Trek*. The group also included 1979 Nobel prizewinner and longtime Hawking friend Steven Weinberg, whose 1977 book, *The First Three Minutes*, had been one of the first to make the Big Bang theory popular.

Over three days, in public lectures and invitation-only panel discussions, the eminent scientists considered the future of cosmology. As they put it to journalists trying to communicate the subject to everyday readers, listeners, and viewers, their task as leading scientists was to understand the origin, the structure, and the fate of the universe. In particular, they intended to learn, at least in theory, how dark matter—the mysteriously invisible but detectable material known to exist both in and between galaxies and that seems to make up most of the cosmos—manages to warp space. At the same time, they were looking for a better understanding of dark energy, the equally mysterious power that, so far as any scientist can tell, keeps pushing the universe apart at a faster and faster rate.

While in Cleveland, Stephen delivered his popular "Brane New World" lecture to a packed auditorium. He also received the Michelson-Morley Award, named for Albert Michelson and Edward Morley, whose experiments at the Case Institute of Technology in 1887 started Einstein thinking about relativity.

As always, Stephen received praise from all attendants of the meeting. Speaking of Stephen's presence at the CERCA conference, Lawrence Krauss said, "Stephen is a remarkable human being and a remarkable scientist. He is without a doubt the most famous scientist alive today, and thus his presence here is a historical event."

Stephen Changes His Mind

On August 21, 2004, Hawking made front-page news when he announced that for 30 years he had been wrong about black holes. He had long insisted that anything ingested by a black hole could never escape from it because its gravity was so powerful.

Now he agreed with other physicists who had always argued that, under the quantum theory, information—that is, any matter—is always preserved. Anything that falls into a black hole, he said, can flow back out into the universe as radiation.

"I'm sorry to disappoint science fiction fans," said Stephen, "but if information is preserved there is no possibility of using black holes to travel to other universes. If you jump into a black hole, your mass energy will be returned to our universe, but in a mangled form,

(Campix)

which contains the information about what you were like, but in an unrecognizable state."

"Quite beautifully normal"

Stephen Hawking is a man whose desire to help the world understand the mysteries of space and time is matched only by his courage in dealing with his own disability. Terri Rozaieski, the wheelchair technician who got to know Stephen when she and her husband delivered his new chair in 2001, put it this way:

> I have always been amazed that of those people we count as heroes, not one of them revels in that title. Rather, they see those things that we label heroic or grandiose as just a part of their lives and in most cases not even the biggest and most important parts. They are those people who, regardless of their most profound accomplishments, remain quite beautifully normal. Dr. Hawking is a man born to teach. His message isn't one of intellectual superiority or incomprehensible theories. Rather, he speaks with great passion about those things which challenge and elevate his mind. And if you watch closely, you will see a spark of excitement and an expression of contentment when he inspires another person to see more clearly the answers to those questions of the universe that once brought only confusion.

TIME LINE

1942   Born on January 8 in Oxford, England

1950   Family moves to St. Albans

1958   Builds LUCE computer

1959   Enters Oxford University

1960   Becomes popular coxswain of Oxford rowing crews

1962   Graduates from Oxford and enters Cambridge University as a graduate student in cosmological research

1963   Diagnosed with amyotrophic lateral sclerosis (ALS), known as "Lou Gehrig's disease"

1965   Graduates from Cambridge with Ph.D.; wins fellowship at Caius College, Cambridge; marries Jane

Wilde; speech on singularity delivered for him at Florida conference

1966 Wins Adams Prize for essay on "Singularities and the Geometry of Spacetime"

1967 Son Robert George Hawking born May 28

1970 First uses wheelchair; daughter Lucy born November 2; joins staff of Institute of Astronomy

1974 Discovers that black holes emit radiation; made a Fellow of the Royal Society; moves to Caltech in Pasadena, California, with family for one year on a Sherman Fairchild Distinguished Scholarship

1977 Gains worldwide publicity from BBC TV program *The Key to the Universe*; offered Chair in Gravitational Physics at Cambridge

1978 Accepts the Albert Einstein Award of the Lewis and Rose Strauss Memorial Fund in Washington, D.C.

1979 Son Timothy Stephen Hawking born on April 15; co-edits *General Relativity: An Einstein Centenary Survey*; appointed Lucasian Professor of Mathematics; made *Man of the Year* by the Royal Association for Disability and Rehabilitation

1981 Attends Pontifical Academy of Sciences in the Vatican; publishes *Superspace and Supergravity* with color cover; appointed a Commander of the British Empire by Queen Elizabeth II

1983 Offered contract for book on cosmology for the general reader; family featured on BBC program *Horizon*

1985 Worldwide lecture tour; windpipe blockage in Switzerland, with tracheostomy in England; awarded grants by John and Catherine MacArthur Foundation; given Equalizer computer program that activates voice synthesizer

1988 Publishes *A Brief History of Time*; discusses religion with actress-metaphysician Shirley MacLaine

1989 Appointed a Companion of Honor by Queen Elizabeth II

1990 Performs in filming of *A Brief History of Time*; separates from Jane; moves in with nurse Elaine Mason

1991 Wheelchair hit by taxi

1992 Film *A Brief History of Time* is released; publishes companion book

1993   Publishes book *Black Holes and Baby Universes*; appears in television commercials for British Telecom (BT)

1995   Marries Elaine Mason

1997   Represents Cambridge University in negotiations with Bill Gates and city of Cambridge; given state-of-the-art computer with GSM system by Intel

1999   Invited by President Clinton to the White House to lecture in "Millennium Evenings" series

2000   Lectures in South Korea, California, Scotland

2001   Lectures in India, Germany, California, Tokyo; gets sophisticated new wheelchair; publishes *The Universe in a Nutshell*

2002   Is acclaimed in celebration of his 60th birthday with four-day "technical scientific workshop"; delivers first "Brane New World" lecture in Portland, Oregon; wins England's Aventis Book Prize; lectures and participates in string-theory conferences in Chinese cities

2003   Lectures by satellite to MIT students; lectures and participates in month-long conference at Texas A&M University; is honored by establishment of

Stephen Hawking Chair at Texas A&M; in Sweden, lectures and participates in six-day Nobel symposium on String Theory and Cosmology; in Cleveland, Ohio, lectures and participates in opening of new Center for Education and Research in Cosmology and Astrophysics (CERCA) at Case Western Reserve University and receives the Michelson-Morley Award; changes his opinion that nothing can escape from a black hole

HOW TO BECOME A COLLEGE PROFESSOR

THE JOB

College and university faculty members teach at junior colleges or at four-year colleges and universities. At four-year institutions, most faculty members are *assistant professors, associate professors,* or *full professors.* These three types of professorships differ in status, job responsibilities, and salary. Assistant professors are new faculty members who are working to get tenure (status as a permanent professor); they seek to advance to associate and then to full professorships.

College professors perform three main functions: teaching, advising, and research. Their most important responsibility is to teach students. Their role within a college department will determine the level of courses they teach and the number of courses per semester. Most professors work with students at all levels, from college freshmen to graduate students. They may head several classes a semester or only a few a year. Some of their classes will have large enrollment, while graduate seminars may consist of only 12 or fewer students. Though college professors may spend fewer than 10 hours a week in the actual classroom, they spend many hours preparing lectures and lesson plans, grading papers and exams, and preparing grade reports. They also schedule office hours during the week to be available to students outside of the lecture hall, and they meet with students individually throughout the semester. In the classroom, professors lecture, lead discussions, administer exams, and assign textbook reading and other research. In some courses, they rely heavily on laboratories to transmit course material.

Another important professorial responsibility is advising students. Not all faculty members serve as advisers, but those who do must set aside large blocks of time to guide students through the program. College professors who serve as advisers may have any number of students assigned to them, from fewer than 10 to more than 100, depending on the administrative policies of the college. Their responsibility may involve looking over a planned program of study to make sure the students meet requirements for graduation, or it may involve working intensively with each student on many aspects of college life.

The third responsibility of college and university faculty members is research and publication. Faculty members who are heavily involved in research programs sometimes are assigned a smaller teaching load. College professors publish their research findings in various scholarly journals. They also write books based on their research or on their own knowledge and experience in the field. Most textbooks are written by college and university teachers. In arts-based programs, such as master's of fine arts programs in painting, writing, and theater, professors practice their craft and exhibit their art work in various ways. For example, a painter or photographer will have gallery showings, while a poet will publish in literary journals.

Publishing a significant amount of work has been the traditional standard by which assistant professors prove themselves worthy of becoming permanent, tenured faculty. Typically, pressure to publish is greatest for assistant professors. Pressure to publish increases again if an associate professor wishes to be considered for a promotion to full professorship.

In recent years, some liberal arts colleges have recognized that the pressure to publish is taking faculty away from their primary duties to the students, and these institutions have begun to place a decreasing emphasis on publishing and more on performance in the classroom. Professors in junior colleges face less pressure to publish than those in four-year institutions.

Some faculty members eventually rise to the position of *department chair,* where they govern the affairs of an entire department, such as English, mathematics, or biological sciences. Department chairs, faculty, and other professional staff members are aided in their myriad duties by *graduate assistants,* who may help develop teaching materials, conduct research, give examinations, teach lower level courses, and carry out other activities.

Some college professors may also conduct classes in an extension program. In such a program, they teach evening and weekend courses for the benefit of people who otherwise would not be able to take advantage of the institution's resources. They may travel away from the campus and meet with a group of students at another location. They may work full time for the extension division or may divide their time between on-campus and off-campus teaching.

Distance learning programs give professors the opportunity to use today's technologies to remain in one place while teaching students who are at a variety of locations simultaneously. The professor's duties, like those when teaching correspondence courses conducted by mail, include grading work that students send in at periodic intervals and advising students of their progress. Computers, the Internet, email, and video conferencing, however, are some of the technology tools that allow professors and students to communicate in "real time" in a virtual classroom setting. Meetings may be scheduled during the same time as traditional classes or during evenings and weekends. Professors who do this work are sometimes known as *extension work, correspondence,* or *distance learning instructors.* They may teach online courses in addition to other classes or may have distance learning as their major teaching responsibility.

The *junior college instructor* has many of the same kinds of responsibilities as the teacher in a four-year college or university. Because junior colleges offer only a two-year program, they teach only undergraduates.

REQUIREMENTS
High School
Follow your high school's college preparatory program, which likely includes courses in English, science, foreign language, history, math, and government. In addition, you should take courses in speech to get a sense of what it will be like to lecture to a group of students. Your

school's debate team can also help you develop public speaking skills, along with research skills.

Postsecondary Training

At least one advanced degree in your field of study is required to be a professor in a college or university. The master's degree is considered the minimum standard, and graduate work beyond the master's is usually desirable. If you hope to advance in academic rank above instructor, most institutions require a doctorate.

In the last year of your undergraduate program, you'll apply to graduate programs in your area of study. Standards for admission to a graduate program can be high and the competition heavy, depending on the school. Once accepted into a program, your responsibilities will be similar to those of your professors—in addition to attending seminars, you'll research, prepare articles for publication, and teach some undergraduate courses.

You may find employment in a junior college with only a master's degree. Advancement in responsibility and in salary, however, is more likely to come if you have earned a doctorate.

Other Requirements

You should enjoy reading, writing, and researching. Not only will you spend many years studying in school, but your whole career will be based on communicating your thoughts and ideas. People skills are important because you'll be dealing directly with students, administrators, and other faculty members on a daily basis. You should feel comfortable in a role of authority and possess self-confidence.

EXPLORING

Your high school teachers use many of the same skills as college professors, so talk to your teachers about their careers and their college experiences. You can develop your own teaching experience by volunteering at a community center, working at a day care center, or working at a summer camp. Also, spend some time on a college campus to get a sense of the environment. Write to colleges for their admissions brochures and course catalogs (or check them out online); read about the faculty members and the courses they teach. Before visiting college campuses, make arrangements to speak to professors who teach courses that interest you. These professors may allow you to sit in on their classes and observe. Also, make appointments with college advisers and with people in the admissions and recruitment offices. If your grades are good enough, you might be able to serve as a teaching assistant during your undergraduate years, which can give you experience leading discussions and grading papers.

EMPLOYERS

Employment opportunities vary based on area of study and education. Most universities have many different departments that hire faculty. With a doctorate, a number of publications, and a record of good teaching, professors should find opportunities in universities all across the country. There are more than 3,800 colleges and universities in the United States. Professors teach in undergraduate and graduate programs. The teaching jobs at doctoral institutions are usually better paying and more prestigious. The most sought-after positions are those that offer tenure. Teachers that have only a master's degree will be limited to opportunities with junior colleges, community colleges, and some small private institutions. There are approximately 1.3 million postsecondary teachers employed in the United States.

STARTING OUT

You should start the process of finding a teaching position while you are in graduate school. The process includes developing a curriculum vitae (a detailed, academic resume), writing for publication, assisting with research, attending conferences, and gaining teaching experience and recommendations. Many students begin applying for teaching positions while finishing their graduate program. For most positions at four-year institutions, you must travel to large conferences where interviews can be arranged with representatives from the universities to which you have applied.

Because of the competition for tenure-track positions, you may have to work for a few years in temporary positions, visiting various schools as an *adjunct professor.* Some professional associations maintain lists of teaching opportunities in their areas. They may also make lists of applicants available to college administrators looking to fill an available position.

ADVANCEMENT

The normal pattern of advancement is from instructor to assistant professor, to associate professor, to full professor. All four academic ranks are concerned primarily with teaching and research. College faculty members who have an interest in and a talent for administration may be advanced to chair of a department or to dean of their college. A few become college or university presidents or other types of administrators.

The instructor is usually an inexperienced college teacher. He or she may hold a doctorate or may have completed all the Ph.D. requirements except for the dissertation. Most colleges look upon the rank of instructor as the period during which the college is trying out the teacher. Instructors usually are advanced to the position of assistant professors within three to four years. Assistant professors are given up to about six years to prove themselves worthy of tenure, and if they do so, they become associate professors. Some professors choose to remain at the associate level. Others strive to become full professors and receive greater status, salary, and responsibilities.

Most colleges have clearly defined promotion policies from rank to rank for faculty members, and many have written statements about the number of years in which instructors and assistant professors may remain in grade. Administrators in many colleges hope to encourage younger faculty members to increase their skills and competencies and thus to qualify for the more responsible positions of associate professor and full professor.

EARNINGS

Earnings vary depending on the departments professors work in, the size of the school, the type of school (for example, public, private, or women's only), and by the level of position the professor holds. In its 2000–01 salary survey, the American Association of University Professors (AAUP) reported the average yearly income for all full-time faculty was $60,000. It also reports that professors averaged the following salaries by rank: full professors, $78,912; associate professors, $57,380; assistant professors, $47,358; and instructors, $35,790. Full professors working in disciplines such as law, business, health professions, computer and information sciences, and engineering have the highest salaries. Lower paying disciplines include visual and performing arts, agricultural studies, education, and communications. The American Association for the Advancement of Science reports that, according to findings from its member salary survey, the median earnings for full professors in the life science fields were approximately $108,000 in 2001. Associate professors in life sciences earned a median of $72,000 that same year.

According to a study by the College and University Professional Association for Human Resources, the average salary in all fields at public institutions was $60,893 for 2001–02. At private colleges, the average was $60,289. Law professors earned top salaries of $107,696 at private colleges, and library science faculty members were near the bottom of the salary scale, earning $44,206 per year.

Many professors try to increase their earnings by completing research, publishing in their field, or teaching additional courses. Professors working on the West Coast and the East Coast of the United States and those working at doctorate-granting institutions tend to have the highest salaries.

Benefits for full-time faculty typically include health insurance and retirement funds and, in some cases, stipends for travel related to research, housing allowances, and tuition waivers for dependents.

WORK ENVIRONMENT

A college or university is usually a pleasant place to work. Campuses bustle with all types of activities and events, stimulating ideas, and a young, energetic population. Much prestige comes with success as a professor and scholar; professors have the respect of students, colleagues, and others in their community.

Depending on the size of the department, college professors may have their own offices, or they may have to share offices with colleagues. Their departments may provide them with computers, Internet access, and research assistants. College professors are also able to do much of their office work at home. They can arrange their schedules around class hours, academic meetings, and the established office hours when they meet with students. Most college teachers work more than 40 hours each week. Although college professors may teach only two or three classes a semester, they spend many hours preparing for lectures, examining student work, and conducting research.

OUTLOOK

The U.S. Department of Labor predicts faster than average employment growth for college and university professors over the next several years. College enrollment is projected to grow due to an increased number of 18- to 24-

year-olds, an increased number of adults returning to college, and an increased number of foreign-born students. In addition, opportunities for college teachers will be good in areas such as engineering, business, computer science, and health science, which offer strong career prospects in the world of work. Retirement of current faculty members will also provide job openings. However, competition for full-time, tenure-track positions at four-year schools will be very strong.

A number of factors threaten to change the way colleges and universities hire faculty. Some university leaders are developing more business-based methods of running their schools, focusing on profits and budgets. This can affect college professors in a number of ways. One of the biggest effects is in the replacement of tenure-track faculty positions with part-time instructors. These part-time instructors include adjunct faculty, visiting professors, and graduate students. Organizations such as the AAUP and the American Federation of Teachers are working to prevent the loss of these full-time jobs, as well as to help part-time instructors receive better pay and benefits. Other issues involve the development of long-distance education departments in many schools. Though these correspondence courses have become very popular in recent years, many professionals believe that students in long-distance education programs receive only a second-rate education. A related concern is about the proliferation of computers in the classroom. Some courses consist only of instruction by computer software and the Internet. The effects of these alternative methods on the teaching profession will be offset somewhat by the expected increases in college enrollment in coming years.

TO LEARN MORE ABOUT COLLEGE PROFESSORS

BOOKS

Goldsmith, John A., John Komlos, and Penny Schine Gold. *The Chicago Guide to Your Academic Career.* Chicago: University of Chicago Press, 2001.

Lyons, Richard E., Marcella L. Kysilka, and George E. Pawlas. *The Adjunct Professor's Guide to Success: Surviving and Thriving in the College Classroom.* Upper Saddle River, N.J.: Allyn and Bacon, 1998.

Peters, Robert L. *Getting What You Came for: The Smart Student's Guide to Earning a Master's or a Ph.D.* Noonday Press, 1997.

ORGANIZATIONS

To read about the issues affecting college professors, contact the following organizations:

American Association of University Professors

1012 14th Street, NW, Suite 500

Washington, DC 20005

Tel: 202-737-5900

Email: aaup@aaup.org

http://www.aaup.org

American Federation of Teachers

555 New Jersey Avenue, NW

Washington, DC 20001

Tel: 202-879-4400

Email: online@aft.org

http://www.aft.org

HOW TO BECOME A PHYSICIST

THE JOB

Physics is the most comprehensive of the natural sciences because it includes the behavior of all kinds of matter, from the smallest particles to the largest galaxies.

Basic, or pure, physics is a study of the behavior of the universe and is organized into a series of related laws. Basic physics can be studied from two points of view: experimental and theoretical. A physicist may work from one or both of these points of view. The *experimental physicist* performs experiments to gather information. The results of the experiments may support or contradict existing theories or establish new ideas where no theories existed before.

The *theoretical physicist* constructs theories to explain experimental results. If the theories are to stand the test of time, they must also predict the results of future experiments. Both the experimental physicist and the theoretical physicist try to extend the limits of what is known.

Not all physicists are concerned with testing or developing new theories. *Applied physicists* develop useful devices and procedures and may hold alternative job titles. Various types of engineers, such as electrical and mechanical engineers, are trained in physics. Applied physics and engineering have led to the development of such devices as television sets, airplanes, washing machines, satellites, and elevators.

Physicists rely heavily on mathematics. Mathematical statements are more precise than statements in words alone. Moreover, the results of experiments can be accurately compared with the various theories only when mathematical techniques are used.

The various laws of physics attempt to explain the behavior of nature in a simple and general way. Even the most accepted laws of physics, however, are subject to change. Physicists continually subject the laws of physics to new tests to see if, under new conditions, they still hold true. If they do not hold true, changes must be made in the laws, or entirely new theories must be proposed.

At the beginning of the 20th century, the laws of physics were tested extensively and found to be too narrow to explain many of the new discoveries. A new body of theories was needed. The older body of laws is called classical physics; the new is called modern physics.

Classical physics is usually divided into several branches, each of which deals with a group of related phenomena. *Mechanics* is the study of forces and their effect on matter. *Hydromechanics* studies the mechanics of liquids and gases. *Optics* is the study of the behavior of light. Physicists in this field study such things as lasers, liquid crystal displays, or light-emitting diodes. *Thermodynamics* is the study of heat. *Acoustics* is the study of sound, such as in recording studio acoustics, underwater sound waves, and electroacoustical devices such as loudspeakers. The study of electricity and magnetism also forms a branch of classical physics. Research in this area includes microwave propagation, the magnetic properties of matter, and electrical devices for science and industry.

Modern physics is also broken up into various fields of study. *Atomic physics* is the study of the structure of atoms and the behavior of electrons, one of the kinds of particles that make up the atom. *Nuclear physics* is the study of the nucleus, or center, of the atom and of the forces that hold the nucleus together. *High-energy physics*, or *particle physics*, is the study of the production of subatomic particles from other particles and energy. The characteristics of these various particles are studied using particle accelerators, popularly called atom smashers.

Solid-state physics is the study of the behavior of solids, particularly crystalline solids. Cryogenic, or low-temperature, techniques are often used in research into the solid state. Research in solid-state physics has produced transistors, integrated circuits, and masers that have improved computers, radios, televisions, and navigation and guidance systems for satellites. *Plasma physics* is the study of the properties of highly ionized gases. Physicists in this field are concerned with the generation of thermonuclear power.

Although biology and geology are separate sciences in their own right, the concepts of physics can also be applied directly to them. Where this application has been made, a new series of sciences has developed. To separate them from their parent sciences, they are known by such names as *biophysics* (the physics of living things) and *geophysics* (the physics of the Earth). Similarly, the sciences of chemistry and physics sometimes overlap in subject matter as well as in viewpoint and procedure, creating *physical chemistry*. In *astrophysics*, the techniques of physics are applied to astronomical observations to determine the properties of celestial objects.

Most physicists are engaged in research, and some combine their research with teaching at the university level.

Some physicists are employed in industries, such as petroleum, communications, manufacturing, and medicine.

REQUIREMENTS

High School

If you are interested in becoming a physicist, take college preparatory courses. Be sure to take as many math and science courses as possible. English skills are important, as you must write up your results, communicate with other scientists, and lecture on your findings. In addition, get as much experience as possible working with computers.

Postsecondary Training

Physicists may have one, two, or three degrees. Physicists at the doctoral level command the jobs with the greatest responsibility, such as jobs in basic research and development. Those at the master's level often work in manufacturing or applied research. Those with a bachelor's degree face the most competition and generally work as technicians in engineering, software development, or other scientific areas.

Some employers in industry are attracted to those with a broad scientific background. With a bachelor's degree in physics or a related science, you may be hired with the intention of being trained on the job in a specialty area. As you develop competency in the special field, you may then consider returning to graduate school to concentrate your study in this particular field.

In addition, some teaching opportunities are available to those with bachelor's degrees at the primary and secondary school level. However, in order to teach at the college level (and even at some secondary schools), you will need an advanced degree. While a master's degree may be acceptable to teach at a junior college, most universities require that professors have their doctorates. Those with a master's degree may obtain a job as an assistant in a physics department in a university while working toward a Ph.D. in physics.

Approximately 507 colleges and universities offer a bachelor's degree in physics, and about 255 schools offer master's and doctoral programs. The American Institute of Physics provides a list of graduate institutions; see the following chapter for contact information.

Certification or Licensing

Those who plan to teach at the secondary school level may be able to obtain a teaching position with a bachelor's degree if they also meet the certification requirements for teaching (established by the state department of education in each state). Because different states have different certification requirements, undergraduates should research the requirements for the state in which they hope to teach.

Other Requirements

Physicists are detail oriented and precise. They must have patience and perseverance and be self-motivated. Physicists should be able to work alone or on research teams.

EXPLORING

If you are interested in a job in physics, talk with your science teachers and research careers in the school library. See if your school offers science clubs, such as a physics or astronomy club, to get involved with others that hold the same interests as you. Participation in science fair projects will give you invaluable insight into theory, experimentation, and the scientific process. If your school does not sponsor science fairs, you may find fairs sponsored by your school district, state, or a science society.

EMPLOYERS

According to the *Occupational Outlook Handbook,* about 9,000 physicists and astronomers work in the United States, most of them in industry, in research and development laboratories, and in teaching. Nearly one-fifth of all physicists work for the federal government, mostly in the Departments of Defense, Energy, and Commerce. Those working in industry jobs may hold a job title other than physicist, such as computer programmer, engineer, or systems developer.

STARTING OUT

The placement office of the college or university from which you obtain a degree will often have listings of jobs available. In addition, many industries send personnel interviewers to college campuses with physics programs to seek out and talk to students who are about to receive degrees. Students should also attend industry, career, and science fairs to find out about job openings and interview opportunities.

Those who are interested in teaching in public schools should apply to several school systems in which they may want to work. Some of the larger school systems also send personnel interviewers to campuses to talk with students who are about to receive degrees in science and who also have acquired the necessary courses in education.

Teaching jobs in universities are often obtained either through the contacts of the student's own faculty members in the degree program or through the placement office of the university.

Jobs with government agencies require individuals to first pass a civil service examination.

ADVANCEMENT

High school physics teachers can advance in salary and responsibility as they acquire experience and advanced degrees. The college or university teacher can advance from assistant to full professor and perhaps to head of the department. Higher rank carries with it additional income and responsibilities.

The research physicist employed by a university advances by handling more responsibility for planning and conducting research programs. Salaries should also increase with experience in research over a period of years.

Physicists in federal government agencies advance in rank and salary as they gain experience. They may reach top positions in which they are asked to make decisions vital to the defense effort or to the safety and welfare of the country.

Scientists employed by industry are usually the highest paid in the profession and with experience can advance to research director positions.

EARNINGS

According to the U.S. Department of Labor, the median salary for physicists was $82,535 in 2000. The lowest paid 10 percent earned $51,680 or less; the highest 10 percent earned over $116,290. Physicists employed by the federal government had median earnings of $86,799 in 2001.

In 2000, median salaries for members of the American Institute of Physics ranged from $60,000 for those with a bachelor's degree to $78,000 for those with a doctorate.

As highly trained and respected scientists, physicists usually receive excellent benefits packages, including health plans, vacation and sick leave, and other benefits.

WORK ENVIRONMENT

Most physicists work a 40-hour week under pleasant circumstances. Laboratories are usually well equipped, clean, well lighted, temperature controlled, and functional. Adequate safety measures are taken when there is any sort of physical hazard involved in the work. Often, groups of scientists work together as a team so closely that their association may last over a period of many years.

Physicists who teach at the high school, college, or university level have the added benefit of following the academic calendar, which gives them ample time away from teaching and meeting with students in order to pursue their own research, studies, or travel.

OUTLOOK

According to the *Occupational Outlook Handbook,* employment for physicists should grow about as fast as the average through 2010. Increases in government research, particularly in the Departments of Defense and Energy, as well as in civilian physics-related research will create more opportunities for physicists. The need to replace retiring workers will account for almost all new job openings.

Opportunities in private industry are plentiful, in areas such as computer technology, semiconductor technology, and other applied sciences.

Job candidates with doctoral degrees have the best outlook for finding work. Graduates with bachelor's degrees are generally underqualified for most physicist jobs. They may find better employment opportunities as engineers, technicians, or computer specialists. With a suitable background in education, they may teach physics at the high school level.

TO LEARN MORE ABOUT PHYSICS AND PHYSICISTS

BOOKS

Brallier, Jess M. *Who Was Albert Einstein?* New York: Grosset & Dunlap, 2002.

Feynman, Richard P. *Six Easy Pieces.* New York: Basic Books, 1996.

Gribbin, John R., and Mary Gribbin. *Eyewitness: Time & Space.* New York: Dorling Kindersley, 2000.

Kuhn, Karl F. *Basic Physics: A Self-Teaching Guide.* Hoboken, N.J.: Wiley, 1996.

MacLachlan, James. *Galileo Galilei: First Physicist.* Oxford Portraits in Science. New York: Oxford, 1999.

ORGANIZATIONS

For employment statistics and information on jobs and career planning, contact

American Institute of Physics
One Physics Ellipse
College Park, MD 20740
Tel: 301-209-3100
Email: aipinfo@aip.org
http://www.aip.org

Fermilab offers internships, learning and employment opportunities, and general information about its laboratory. For more information, contact

Fermi National Accelerator Laboratory
Education Office
PO Box 500
Batavia, IL 60510
Tel: 630-840-3000
http://www.fnal.gov

For career information and employment opportunities in Canada, contact

Canadian Association of Physicists
Suite 112, MacDonald Building
150 Louis Pasteur Avenue
Ottawa, ON K1N 6N5 Canada

Tel: 613-562-5614

Email: cap@physics.uottawa.ca

http://www.cap.ca

For information on federal employment, check out the following website:

USA Jobs

http://www.usajobs.opm.gov

TO LEARN MORE ABOUT STEPHEN HAWKING

BOOKS

Boslough, John. *Beyond the Black Hole: Stephen Hawking's Universe.* London: Fontana, 1985.

Coles, Peter. *Hawking and the Mind of God.* New York: Totem Books, 2000.

Ferguson, Kitty. *Stephen Hawking: Quest for a Theory of Everything.* New York: Bantam, 1992.

Gribbin, John. *In Search of the Big Bang.* New York: Penguin, 1999.

———. *In Search of the Edge of Time.* New York: Penguin, 1999.

Gribbin, John and Mary. *Richard Feynman: A Life in Science*. London: Viking, 1997.

Hawking, Jane. *Music to Move the Stars*. London: Pan Books, 2000.

Hawking, Stephen. *A Brief History of Time*. New York: Bantam, 1996.

———. *The Illustrated Brief History of Time*. London: Bantam, 1996.

———. *The Universe in a Nutshell*. New York: Bantam, 2001.

Lightman, Alan, and Roberta Brawer. *Origins: The Lives and Worlds of Modern Cosmologists*. Cambridge, Mass.: Harvard, 1990.

McDaniel, Melissa. *Stephen Hawking: Revolutionary Physicist*. Philadelphia: Chelsea House, 1994.

Overbye, Dennis. *Lonely Hearts of the Cosmos*. Boston: Little, Brown, 1999.

Thorne, Kip. *Black Holes and Time Warps*. New York: Norton, 1994.

White, Michael, and John Gribbin. *Stephen Hawking: A Life in Science*. Washington: Joseph Henry Press, 2002.

WEBSITES

"Professor Stephen Hawking's Homepage." Available online. URL: http://www.hawking.org.uk.html. Downloaded September 7, 2003.

"Professor Stephen Hawking Stays Connected to the World Through the Latest Intel Technology," Intel website. Available online. URL: http://www.intel.com/ pressroom/archive/releases/CN032097.HTM#top. Downloaded September 7, 2003.

"Science in the Future," background information for Dr. Hawking's appearance in Mumbai, India, January 2001. Available online. URL: http://theory.tifr.res.in/strings/ index.html. Downloaded September 7, 2003.

"Lecture at USC," background information for Dr. Hawking's appearance at University of Southern California Santa Barbara, February/March 2002. Available online. URL: http://citmsc.usc.edu/hawking/. Downloaded September 7, 2003.

"Conversations with Dr. Hawking," Pride Mobility Products Corporation website. Available online. URL://www. pridemobility.com/pridewebtalk/Stephen_Hawking/. Downloaded September 7, 2003.

"Happy 60th Birthday," Cambridge University Department of Applied Mathematics and Theoretical Physics (DAMTP) press release. Available online. URL: http://www.damtp.cam.ac.uk/user/hawking60/. Posted January 2, 2002.

"Pope Named to Stephen Hawking Chair at Texas A&M," *Aggie Daily* (Texas A&M newspaper). Available online.

URL:http://www.tamu.edu/univrel/aggiedaily/news/stories/02/103002-10.html. Posted October 30, 2002.

"Hawking muses on ultimate theory of the universe," Massachusetts Institute of Technology (MIT) press release. Available online. URL: http://www.mit.edu/newsoffice/nr/2003/hawking2.html. Posted January 23, 2003.

"Stephen Hawking, Famed Physicist and Author, to Present Public Speeches at Texas A&M and The Woodlands," *Aggie Daily* (Texas A&M newspaper). URL: http://www.tamu.edu/univrel/aggiedaily/news/stories/03/030603-6.html. Posted March 6, 2003.

"String Theory and Cosmology," Nobel Symposium, Sigtuna, Sweden, press release. Available online. URL: http://www.nobel.se/physics/symposia/ns127/about.html. Downloaded September 7, 2003.

Mangels, John. "Great minds to ponder path of cosmology while in town," *The Plain Dealer*, Cleveland, Ohio. Available online. URL: http://genesis1.phys.cwru.edu/~krauss/cosmostory.html. Posted October 6, 2003.

Pease, Roland. "Brane new world," *Nature* magazine, June 28, 2001. Available online. URL: http://nature.com/cgi-taf/DynaPage.taf?file=nature/journal/v411/n6841/full/411986a0_r.html. Posted June 28, 2001.

Podojil, Catherine, "Physicist Stephen Hawking joins Case conference," *Cleveland Free Times*. Available online.

URL: http://admission.cwru.edu/admissions/news/ news_story.asp?Inewsid = 243&strBack = %2Fadmissions%2Fnews%2Fnews_archive.asp. Posted October 12, 2003.

Rozaieski, Terri, "On Meeting a Hero. . ." Pride Mobility Products Corporation website. Available online. URL: http://www.pridemobility.com/pridewebtalk/Stephen _Hawking/Meeting_a_Hero/meeting_a_hero.html. Downloaded September 7, 2003.

Thaller, Michelle. "Gravity: Strength in Weakness," *Christian Science Monitor*, September 24, 2003. Available online. URL: http://www.csmonitor.com/2003/0924/ p25s01-stss.htm. Posted September 24, 2003.

COSMOLOGY AND PHYSICS GLOSSARY

atom   basic element of all matter in the universe, consisting of a tiny nucleus made of protons and neutrons surrounded by orbiting electrons; any atom is roughly half protons and half neutrons

Big Bang   theory describing the origin and evolution of the cosmos

black hole   region or sector of spacetime in which Hawking believed, until he changed his mind in 2004, gravity is so strong that not even light can escape from it

brane theory   theory that the vast universe has more than four dimensions (three of space and one of time);

derived from the word "membrane," meaning a two-dimensional surface that comes between two three-dimensional volumes of space, it assumes that our universe may function as a sort of membrane in space between even greater volumes of space that contain more than four dimensions of spacetime

cosmology study of the entire universe

electron particle that has a negative electrical charge and orbits the nucleus of an atom

general relativity Einstein's theory first published in 1916; proposes that space and time are relative and cannot be dealt with separately, and that the presence of mass can warp or distort space

Hawking Radiation radiation from a black hole that occurs when a pair of virtual particles is produced near the black hole's edge or horizon and one falls into the hole while the other escapes into space.

neutron one of the particles of an atom; has no electrical charge; neutrons and protons make up the nucleus of an atom; each neutron consists of three smaller particles called quarks

nucleus center of an atom, made up of neutrons and protons

photon particle that has no mass and that moves at the speed of light; when we see light, we are seeing photons;

when we use radio waves, microwaves, gamma rays, or X rays, we are using invisible photons

Planck's constant   German theoretical physicist Max Karl Ernst Ludwig Planck developed the principle that any radiant energy, such as light, radio waves, or X rays, is made up of extremely tiny bits of energy that cannot be reduced smaller than a constant size

proton   like neutrons, protons are particles that make up the nucleus of an atom, and each proton consists of three smaller particles called quarks; unlike neutrons, protons have a positive electrical charge.

pulsar   neutron star that rotates rapidly and creates radio waves with a regular pulse; the pulse rate may be several hundred or several thousand times per second

quark   fundamental particle (fundamental means that it cannot be divided into anything tinier); in groups of three, quarks make up neutrons and protons

quantum physics   study of the extremely small, such as the atom or its even smaller properties

quasar   an object in space that is similar to a star but has tremendous energy and is at least 100 million times the size of our sun

singularity   point of infinite density; theorists believe that the center of a black hole contains a singularity and that the Big Bang exploded from a singularity

spacetime   the three dimensions of space, and the one dimension of time, combined

string theory   idea that particles consist of waves like strings that have no dimension other than length

supernova   vast explosion of a star that leaves behind its inner core as the material blown away forms the basic elements of new planets and stars

wormhole   in spacetime, a tunnel or tube that connects areas of our universe or links other universes to ours; theorists believe that wormholes can make time travel possible

INDEX

Page numbers in *italics* indicate illustrations.